Elements of Article Writing Series

STRUCTURE & FLOW

DAVID A. FRYXELL

WRITER'S DIGEST BOOKS
CINCINNATI, OHIO

Structure & Flow. Copyright © 1996 by David Fryxell. Printed and bound in the United States of America. All rights reserved. No part of this book may be reproduced in any form or by any electronic or mechanical means including information storage and retrieval systems without permission in writing from the publisher, except by a reviewer, who may quote brief passages in a review. Published by Writer's Digest Books, an imprint of F&W Publications, Inc., 1507 Dana Avenue, Cincinnati, Ohio 45207. (800) 289-0963. First edition.

Portions of this book have appeared, in a different form, in *Writer's Digest* magazine.

This hardcover edition of *Structure & Flow* features a "self-jacket" that eliminates the need for a separate dust jacket. It provides sturdy protection for your book while it saves paper, trees and energy.

Other fine Writer's Digest Books are available from your local bookstore or direct from the publisher.

00 99 98 97 96 5 4 3 2 1

Library of Congress Cataloging-in-Publication Data

Fryxell, David A.
    Structure & flow / David A. Fryxell—1st ed.
        p.   cm.—(Elements of article writing series)
    ISBN 0-89879-705-5
    1. Authorship. I. Title. II. Series.
PN147.F78   1996
808'.02—dc20   95-50553
                                                                 CIP

Edited by Jack Heffron and Roseann S. Biederman
Cover and interior designed by Sandy Kent

For Courtney,
the *next* writer in the family

TABLE OF CONTENTS

Part One
ORDER OUT OF CHAOS

Part Two
THE PIECES

𝒫art 𝒯hree

PUTTING THE PIECES TOGETHER

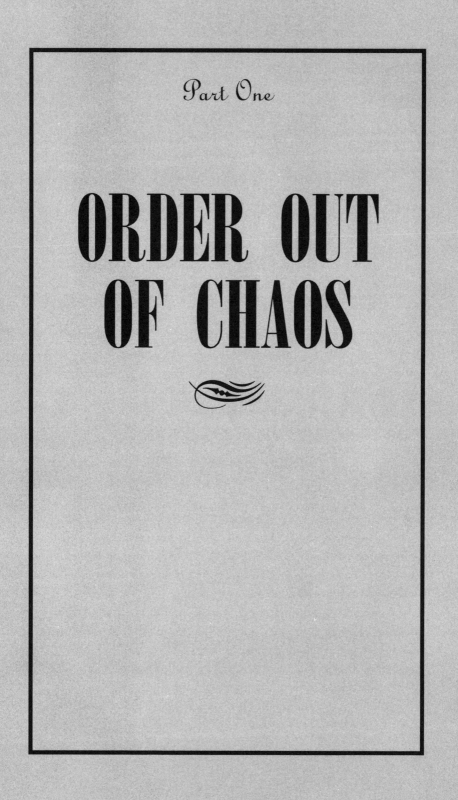

Part One

ORDER OUT OF CHAOS

CHAPTER ONE

The Shape of Nonfiction

Making life into art

When I was a kid, one of my favorite comic book heroes was, of course, Superman. I admired his ability to fly and figured that his knack for bouncing bullets off his chest might come in handy in a pinch. But what I really envied was Superman's trick of turning a lump of coal into a diamond simply by squeezing it in his super fist. It wasn't that instant diamonds would take the sting out of paying the light bill and the mortgage (I was a kid—what did I know or care about bills?); no, I think at some deeper level I was impressed by Superman's ability to turn the plainest raw material into something precious and beautiful. Leaping tall buildings in a single bound is a nice party trick, but making diamonds out of coal—now that's *super*.

Of course, making diamonds out of coal is what the nonfiction writer does every day, every time he sits down before a blank page or an empty screen. The messy world of facts, squeezed into the writer's notebook, is the coal; the writer's art consists of selecting and shaping that raw material into something precious and beautiful.

And what's the difference between a lump of coal and a diamond? The transformation requires no alchemy—both coal and diamond are humble carbon. The difference between a lump of coal and a diamond, as Superman and eighth-grade science students know, is *structure*.

The Basic Dictionary of Science defines a diamond as "carbon present naturally in the earth in the form of crystals, generally with eight three-sided faces." It's the diamond's crystalline structure that makes it, as the definition goes on to note, "the hardest natural substance, used in industry for cutting, etc., and highly valued as a jewel stone because of its brilliance."

Similarly, the nonfiction writer traffics not in metamorphosis but in synthesis, performing not alchemy but orchestration. The carbon is still carbon; the words remain mere words. Yet, magically (it seems), the nonfiction writer takes what is "naturally present" and, by the choices he makes in selection and structure, turns it into something "highly valued" and "brilliant."

Guy de Maupassant described the writer's challenge as "not to give us a banal photograph of life, but rather to give us the most complete, impressive and convincing vision of life—more than reality itself is." In short, to take the raw material of life and squeeze and shape it into art, into something that is of and yet finer than the shapeless and disorderly world around us. Order out of chaos, that's the job at hand and the purpose of structure and form.

Structure and form make diamonds out of coal, a thing of beauty from a spiderweb, a symphony out of a babel of notes, a work of art from the confusion of the modern world.

The carpentry of nonfiction

And yet, for all the words that have been written about writing, no one talks much about the structural task of writing. Perhaps that's because a *task* is exactly what it is—hard work requiring discipline and as much a logician's head for analysis as a poet's heart. Those who like to talk about writing would rather dwell on the romance of it all, the drama of reporting: Ernie Pyle on the battlefield, George Plimpton in the bullring, Woodward and Bernstein in the parking garage with Deep Throat. Or they will gladly share with you the artful agony of writer's block (hey, talking about writing is a great way to avoid *doing* it), the pangs of waiting for *le mot juste* to pop into the haggard author's head. Structure sounds too much like carpentry, which is about as romantic as banging your thumb with a hammer.

Yet the structure of writing can be, must be, art as well as craft, just as architecture—another business that's all about structure and form—

is about art as much as it is about putting up skyscrapers that won't fall down. "Art is nothing without form," wrote Gustave Flaubert. The writer Florence King put it still more bluntly: "Discipline is never a restraint [on creativity]. It's an aid. The first commandment of the romantic school is: 'Don't worry about grammar, spelling, punctuation, vocabulary, plot or structure—just let it come.' That's not writing; that's vomiting, and it leads to uncontrolled, unreadable prose."

After all, structure is not just a matter of what part of the story goes where; it's also about making the assembled whole more than the sum of its parts. This is where the nuts-and-bolts analysis side of structure meets its yin-yang opposite, synthesis—putting the parts together to make a whole. As Andy Rooney, of all people, once put it, "The business of any artwork—if I can refer to my stuff generally as art—is synthesis. If you have a novel, the idea is to condense it and get something said in less time than it took to live it."

If you have nonfiction instead of a novel, he might have added, synthesis is even more important. In fiction, at least, part of the process is the generation of material—making stuff up, in other words. Writing fiction involves drawing out from within, and the more vividly the writer can imagine, the more powerful the novel or short story. But in nonfiction, synthesis is all: The writer must select from without, from all the possibilities of the real world throughout history and geography.

Nonfiction's power derives almost solely from the artful selection and arrangement of reality. Here, the materials are what the writer has at hand or can rustle up; if the world gives you a bundle of sticks, your challenge is to build the best darned house of sticks (or bridge of sticks—the form, after all, is up to you) that you can, to craft a house of sticks that will make the world gasp in awe. And the wonder, at least to my taste, is all the greater because you did it with what you had, with sticks.

Writing nonfiction is the business, in other words, of imposing structure on a world of fact that too often seems lamentably unstructured. But that is the beauty of the challenge facing the nonfiction writer: However hectic and out of control the world we live in may be, you are given the opportunity to coax meaning out of it all.

Is that really such a chore? Such "carpentry," it seems to me, can be the finest part of putting words on paper. By comparison, the rest of writing seems like mere filling in the blanks.

The form that maximizes your material

So I don't think it's chance that William Strunk, in setting out eleven rules of composition in his classic *The Elements of Style*, chose this rule for number one: "Choose a suitable design and hold to it."

The writer Paul Johnson (quoted in *Good Advice on Writing*, collected by William Safire and Leonard Safir) was more explicit about the importance of "choosing a suitable design" to writing: "Structure is everything. When authors come to me complaining of writer's block, it means that they are too lazy to work out a structure either in their lives or in their work."

Every piece of writing has a structure to it, whether an artful, intentional one or a lazy, meandering mess. A letter to your mother might have a simple, three-part structure:

1. The salutation: *Hi, how are you doing?*
2. The report: *Here's what's new with me.*
3. The closing: *Hope all is well with you; write soon.* (Or: *Send money!*)

A child's report on "What I did on my summer vacation" might resemble a grocery list in structure:

1. I went to the beach.
2. I went to the zoo.
3. I watched cartoons.

. . . and so on.

The recounting of an anecdote or a writeup of a police incident might resemble the basic form of fiction:

1. This happened first.
2. This happened next.

. . . and so on until:

This happened last.

More complex forms of nonfiction may resemble other familiar forms of fiction. A nonfiction story, just like a fictional story, might start with a complicating incident or dramatic moment, flash back to reveal how this came to be, then march forward through the chronology of events until a resolution. (In fact, as we will see, this can be a highly effective structure to adapt to basic article writing.)

Other forms are unique to nonfiction, for good or ill. No novelist, for example, would construct his work in the "inverted pyramid" form so popular in newspapers (see the next chapter for more on the inverted pyramid). On the other hand, the architecture of some articles is more complex and more powerful in its effect than the work of all but the finest fictionalists.

The goal of the nonfiction writer who aspires to art, of course, is to find the form that maximizes his material—that brings out the diamond hidden, all potential, in the coal. John McPhee, the *New Yorker* writer whose work exemplifies the art of making something wonderful out of the plainest subject matter (oranges, rocks, roadkill), once explained it this way: "The piece of writing has a structure inside it. It begins, goes along somewhere, and ends in a manner that is thought out beforehand. I always know the last line of a story before I've written the first one. Going through all that creates the form and shape of the thing."

Cooking up "architectonics"

The highfalutin' term for "the form and the shape of the thing" in nonfiction writing is *architectonics*, which Norman Sims, in his anthology *The Literary Journalists,* defines as "the structural design that gives order, balance and unity to a work, the element of form that relates the parts to each other and to the whole."

Jon Franklin, the first writer to win the Pulitzer Prize for feature writing, likens the architectonic part of the writing process to getting ready to climb a mountain. "Structuring is the art of planning and analysis, of hiring Sherpas, accumulating equipment and buying tickets," he says in *Writing for Story.* "It is the antithesis of dream, as unartful as anything the writer does. Yet it is absolutely necessary to his survival."

Another Pulitzer Prize winner, Richard Rhodes, has observed, in *The Literary Journalists,* "The kind of architectonic structures that you have to build, that nobody ever teaches or talks about, are crucial to writing and have little to do with verbal abilities. They have to do with pattern ability and administrative abilities—generalship, if you will. Writers don't talk about it much, unfortunately."

Seeing, sorting, seeking threads—these are the skills that architectonics demands. In building structures, the nonfiction writer must both separate his materials and find commonalities among seemingly disparate elements.

Though comparisons to architecture and even military strategy are more colorful, it's maybe easiest to understand architectonics by thinking of cooking. I like to cook, particularly spicy Cajun dishes that flirt with inedibility, and I think cooking appeals to me in part because it's like writing. First you assemble the ingredients—onion, chicken breasts, and so on—just as when you write an article you must first gather all your research. But you wouldn't just dump all the onions or all the chicken you've got in the kitchen into your pot any more than you'd put every quote in your notebook into an article. No, the cooking begins with selection: so much onion, this many chicken breasts, just enough cayenne pepper. And you don't add all the ingredients to the stew all at once. In making a good gumbo, for example, there's an order to every ingredient: Some of the onions go into the hot, penny-colored *roux* right away; others are added later, to preserve more of their individual onion identity. Finally, there's a certain style in how the dish is served. You don't just holler "Come and get it!" and slop the stuff into the first dish, bowl or coffee mug that's at hand. With gumbo, you mound a cupful of rice and then carefully ladle the stew on top and all around. With an article, you try to serve up a pleasing presentation that will entice the reader to take that all-important first bite.

Sounds delicious, you're probably saying, but what's it have to do with structure? Seems as though by the time it's served, the onions and chicken and such are all just *gumbo*, and the diner seeking structure would have about as much luck as hunting polar bear in a bayou.

That's the point precisely, of course: to blend the ingredients so skillfully into a larger whole that collectively they become something more delectable than a teaspoon of this or a cup of that. You don't want the reader to see the structure any more than the chef wants the diner back in his kitchen. The process is organized and highly disciplined; the product is pure gumbo.

How to make it "just cookbook"

As any chef will tell you, *haute cuisine* is hard work. It's not the chopping and the mixing that taxes the cook, however; it's the planning and decision making—should it be duck with raspberry vinaigrette or *strawberry* vinaigrette? Truffles or shiitake mushrooms? Marzipan or mousse?

Similarly, let's not pretend that the architectonics of nonfiction writing are anything but brain-straining work—though practice and the principles we'll discuss in this book can make the brainwork come more naturally. Joe McGinnis, author of *Going to Extremes* and *Fatal Vision*, says the organizational challenges before he ever sits down to write are "the hardest part of every book. . . . What do you put in, what do you leave out?" He warns: "It can paralyze you."

But there's a bright side: Once you have finally, even painfully settled on a "recipe" for your article or book, the rest of your writing work goes much more smoothly than if you hadn't taken the time to wrestle with structure in advance. You know the phrase, "it's just cookbook"? With the hardest part of the process behind you, you'll find the actual putting-words-on-paper is almost mechanical, freeing your creative powers to concentrate on finding just the right word and crafting the perfect phrase. It's the difference between tasting to see if there's just enough pepper and deciding whether the dish should have pepper at all, or maybe tarragon instead.

McGinnis, for example, finally found this pattern for his book on Alaska, *Going to Extremes*: He organized his material from cold to warmth, from darkness to light, "from those whose lives were screwed up by Alaska to those who were fulfilled." And once he'd hit on that architectonic principle, the book began to fall into place. A project as big as the largest state could be chopped into manageable bits and then mixed together into a book.

Finding the "shape" of a piece of nonfiction, says John McPhee, "relieves the writer . . . to concentrate each day on one thing. You know right where it fits." Wave goodbye to writer's block. Say hello to pain-free productivity. Now, isn't that worth a little investment upfront?

Understanding structure pays other dividends besides peace of mind, of course. Obviously, it brings order and unity to your work. Your lead, your hook (or "grabber" or "nut graf"—see chapter eleven), those tricky transitions, and even your ending will all flow naturally from your underlying organization. Because your writing is a seamless whole, it more readily wins and sustains reader interest—

that sense of "I couldn't put it down."

This book will show you how to reap these benefits, how to use the secrets of structure and form to solve the problems of leads and endings, focus and angle, exposition and rhythm. It will show you how to master the architectonics of your nonfiction, starting with simple structures and progressing to more complex forms.

We will see, in other words, how to make diamonds out of coal. Trust me: Anyone can do it, even if you're not from the planet Krypton.

CHAPTER TWO

Simple Structures and Beyond

Unlearning the inverted pyramid

The first thing you learn in most journalism courses is probably the first thing you should forget when you set out to write serious nonfiction. If you've never formally studied journalism, perhaps you can be spared this particular bit of unlearning—although it's so deeply ingrained in how we think about nonfiction writing that you might still need a bit of reverse brainwashing.

I'm talking, of course, about the "inverted pyramid," that dictum of Journalism 101 that teaches you to cram all the most important facts into the first paragraph, then unreel the rest of your facts in decreasing order of importance. It's a standby of the old school of newspaper writing. Overzealously applied, the inverted pyramid led to stories that began with indigestible globs of who-what-when-where-why, constipated sentences that defied the reader to read them:

HOOTERVILLE (AP)—A collision between a chicken truck, driven by Edward G. Bumpkin, 46, of rural Hicktown, and a pig truck, driven by Bob "Hog" McTrough, 43, of 2344 Sowview Lane, Hooterville, backed up traffic for six miles late yesterday afternoon on Highway 147 between the Bugtown interchange and the Hooterville exit ramp, where the accident occurred at about 2:30 p.m. when the truck driven by Bumpkin swerved to miss a wandering cow and plowed into McTrough's late-model GMC vehicle. . . .

And—*gasp!*—so on.

Though the inverted pyramid could be carried to ridiculous, not to mention impenetrable extremes, this form made perfect sense for its time. Back then (not quite in the time of the pyramids, despite the name), newspapers were composed on the fly using unforgiving type technologies. Those who made up the pages had neither the time nor the tools to mess with the niceties of structure or transitions; they had to be able to "cut from the bottom," lopping off the rest of a story when the room ran out. So the most important facts had to be kept up front, lest they wind up on the cutting-room floor. And the inverted pyramid was born, named not for its epoch but for its structural shape:

The most important facts went here: who, what, when, where, how
Then came the next most important facts in the story
Followed by the next most important
And still some more facts
That could just be
Cut if need
be.

But remember that the genesis of the inverted pyramid was technological and typographical; any rationalization that this was the way readers preferred to get their material was just that, rationalization in the name of necessity.

Today, offset printing, computerized typography and desktop publishing have made the inverted pyramid obsolete. Not only magazines but, increasingly, newspapers can make stories fit using high-tech trims. And, in this age of CNN and Court TV, newspapers are jettisoning the vestiges of the inverted pyramid in search of ways to better analyze and put into perspective the headlines that readers have likely already seen on TV.

But the inverted pyramid wasn't all wrong. For whatever the wrong reasons, it had its heart in the right place: Get the most important information (well, enough of it to keep 'em reading) to the reader early on. If you retain that lesson while you're unlearning the inverted pyramid, all those old typesetters won't have labored in vain.

From pyramid to hourglass

In fact, the inverted pyramid makes a good starting place for a tour of some of the most basic—and most useful—forms of nonfiction. You can take that old pyramid, give it a few twists, and create basic, useful structures for your articles.

For example, the next form that most journalism students learn is what's sometimes called the "spiral." Think of it as two intertwining inverted pyramids, or as a pair of exceptionally polite pyramids taking turns. While your story would still start with the most important facts about subject A, the next paragraph would introduce the key facts about a second but related subject, B.

Let's say the story is about a fire. You need to communicate: (A) The terrible damage of the fire and (B) the firefighters' valiant efforts to control it. So your story might start like this:

A. The basic facts of the fire damage, the location of the fire, and the time

B. How many firefighters responded to the alarm and how long it took them to douse the fire

The story then "spirals" from there, roughly alternating (in descending order of importance, according to good ol' inverted pyramid rules) between facts about the fire and details of the battle against it:

A. How the fire started
B. How the firefighters attacked it
A. Reactions of the stunned homeowners
B. Reactions of the exhausted firefighters

And so on. Just as with the inverted pyramid, a lazy editor could whack off the bottom of a spiral story and be sure that the key facts would still make it into print. But the story's alternating structure gives it a rhythm that's more pleasing (and interesting) to read and presents the facts in two complementary streams rather than one torrent.

Of course, neither the inverted pyramid nor the spiral represents the way you'd tell a story if you were talking to a friend. If you'd seen the fire firsthand and were talking it through rather than writing it down, you'd probably tell it in simple chronological order: First the fire started . . . then the alarm sounded . . . then the firefighters came . . . and after it was all over this is what was left of the house.

Most of today's nonfiction borrows from this even older, oral storytelling form and relies on chronology to tell part of the story (such as the background leading up to the events in the lead).

Take the form that magazine-writing guru Peter Jacobi calls the "hourglass," for example. An hourglass is a story that starts as an inverted pyramid or a spiral and then switches to a chronological, narrative form. So our story about the fire might begin the same way:

A. The basic facts of the fire damage, the location of the fire, and the time

B. How many firefighters responded to the alarm and how long it took for them to douse the fire

But then, once these fundamental facts are introduced, the hourglass story takes up the tale from the first spark, following it chronologically until the last ashes and interweaving threads A and B as necessary to tell it as it happened:

A. How the fire started

B. How the alarm was sounded

B. How many firefighters responded

B. How the firefighters attacked the fire

B. How they finally put out the fire

A. More details about the damage that was left

B. Reactions of the exhausted firefighters

A. Reactions of the stunned homeowners after the firefighters depart

The hourglass gets its name from the two parts of the form—like the top (the key facts in the beginning) and the bottom (the chronology) of an hourglass, with the story running like sand in between. It combines the virtues of the inverted pyramid or spiral structure with those of the traditional narrative, grabbing the reader with the most important facts and then filling in the rest of the tale in clear, straightforward style.

Investing in structure

Unfortunately, the most important facts aren't necessarily the most interesting facts. If you're looking to catch the reader's attention and draw him into your article, giving him both barrels at the beginning may not be the best strategy. Indeed, having gleaned the key information in the first few paragraphs, the reader may rightly figure it's all downhill from here and skip the rest of your writing.

The lead, after all, is a kind of seduction. You want to tease the reader into making a commitment, not greet him at the door stark naked.

If you replace the barrage of facts at the top of the hourglass with an intriguing sampling of information, you might have a form that gets your story rolling without going downhill too quickly. Then, at the narrow point of the hourglass, give the reader a clear, irresistible promise that the rest of the journey will be worth making. And make sure the chronology that follows lives up to that promise.

That's as close to a surefire structure for a basic magazine article as I can imagine. Ironically, it's a crude description of a model article form found in that birthplace of the inverted pyramid, the newspaper. Specifically, *The Wall Street Journal.*

Yes, *The Wall Street Journal.* I realize that when you think of *The Wall Street Journal,* you see a guide to investing the fruits of your writing, or an update for the barons of capitalism. You think of its strength as statistics in column after column of agate, not as words artfully arranged.

Yet if you're seeking a basic article structure to emulate, there's no better place to look every weekday than the middle column of *The Wall Street Journal.* The left and right parts of the page may appeal to latterday J.P. Morgans, but the Middle Column delivers gems of storytelling on subjects far from Wall Street. (For an instructive collection of these articles, seek out a tall, skinny book with the mouthful title, *Dressing for Dinner in the Naked City and Other Tales from The Wall Street Journal's "Middle Column,"* edited by Jane Berentson.)

Just like the inverted pyramid, the article formula epitomized in the Middle Column presumably evolved out of the restrictions of the newspaper format and story length; yet, as the column's sweep of subject matter proves, it's readily adaptable. Let's dissect it and see.

Grabbing readers in the middle

Start with the lead, which must grab readers from the gray of the newspaper page. Often the Middle Column leads rely on contrast or surprise, the juxtaposition of two elements not ordinarily linked: a convent and the stuffing of pimentos into olives, sea slugs and orgies, a "crummy little theater" in Malibu getting an agitated phone call from Warren Beatty, demanding that his latest film make the marquee. (These are actual articles—now you can't wait to read them, right?) This collision of opposites gives the story its angle and sets up what the rest of the article must explain and explore.

Other Middle Column stories begin by setting a scene: an old gorilla, teeth falling out and toes curled with arthritis, displays a still-healthy appetite . . . a poacher fires a slingshot into the mist . . . four vocational-school students arrive by limo at the school's first prom in decades. . . . The scenes or anecdotes must be powerful enough to catch the casual reader's attention. Often, if more subtly, they rely on the same power of contrast to build their take-off: debilitated gorilla/healthy appetite; modern-day poacher/ancient weapon; fancy limo and prom/workaday vocational school.

Unlike the classic inverted pyramid, this form doesn't require that you pack all the most important facts into the opening. It's more concerned with engaging the reader than with making life easier for the newspaper make-up editor.

On the other hand, these aren't simple narratives: They rarely begin at the chronological beginning of the story. The story about olive stuffing at a former convent starts with pimento production underway, not with the founding of the convent. The prom story opens with students disembarking at the dance, not with them renting the limo.

While not a traditional 1-2-3 narrative, neither is this exactly a bold new idea. It's a storytelling principle as old as Homer: *in medias res*— "in the middle of things"—the Greeks called it. Begin your narrative just as things start to get interesting—with the poacher firing his slingshot into the mist—and you can always wind back around to how this intriguing situation came to pass.

We'll talk a lot more about chronology in chapter twelve. But the secret of this basic but powerful form isn't just putting things in a more interesting order; it's also making a promise to the reader that this story really will be worth reading on to the end.

Setting the hook

That promise is what I like to call the "hook," and what newspaper editors typically call the "nut graf." The hook puts the lead in context—as not just a random collision of opposites or a mere shock for sensation's sake, but as an example of something broader and bigger. The hook makes clear why the reader should keep reading and sets the theme or focus of the story. It makes a promise that what follows must deliver on.

So the story of the aging gorilla, for example, becomes an article by *Journal* reporter Francine Schwadel about the *world's oldest* gorilla— who, when it dies, will be examined by scientists for clues to the aging process. The hand-stuffing of olives at a former convent (18 olives a minute), described by one of my favorite *Journal* writers, Barry Newman, epitomizes the old method of pimento production that is giving way to mechanization (1,800 olives a minute)—but at what cost in flavor and texture? The crummy little Malibu theater stands out among 23,814 screens in America, as reporter Richard Turner tells it, because of its proximity to where the stars live; at Oscar time, movie stars gather to honor the films that many of them first saw here, at the Malibu Theater. No wonder Warren Beatty is agitated!

We'll examine this crucial "who cares?" element in detail in chapter eleven. For now, let's follow the Middle Column structure as it unfolds to deliver on the promise of the lead and hook.

Next, typically, several more paragraphs elaborate on the hook or present necessary background information. What does science hope to learn from the world's oldest gorilla? Why do celebrities opt for the Malibu Theater? What's the impact, economic and gustatory, of the change in pimento stuffing?

It's easy to see why the paragraphs following the hook are a good place for filling in the details: You've just seized the reader's attention and convinced him of the importance or interest of your story, so if ever there's a place to coast—just a little—it's here. The reader won't expect more fireworks or cosmic concepts, at least not for a few paragraphs. Rather, the reader would like to know anything else that's essential to understanding the story to come.

Of course, whatever comes after the hook must be just as essential to the story. If it doesn't fit your focus (a topic we'll explore in chapter four), if it doesn't help deliver on your angle, leave it out—no matter how interesting or charming or cleverly phrased. Imagine your copy going under the knife of ruthless *Wall Street Journal* editors, impatient with anything that unnecessarily keeps their readers from making money!

Pretty quickly, then, the Middle Column stories get back to the chronology begun with the lead. Here, though, is the chronological—as opposed to the dramatic—start of the story. It's 1930 and the world's-oldest-gorilla-to-be is born in Africa. . . . Or it's just last fall, and a young entrepreneur buys a fading Malibu movie theater . . . .

It may be a long trek from the chronological beginning to the dramatic point of the lead (multiple paragraphs tracing the gorilla's capture and unusual growing up among humans). Or it may take only a quick burst of a few paragraphs from the chronology's start (buying the movie theater) to the scene in the lead (Warren Beatty calls). The length of this segment depends on the complexity of the chronology and its importance to the focus.

Sooner or later, the story must catch up with itself. If you were to diagram the sequence of events as they are presented, it might look like this: D (the dramatic lead in the middle of things), A (the chronological start of the story), B, C, back to D, E, F and so on. If you can find that dramatic point—D in this example—and then bring the reader back around to it, the rest of the narrative should roll off your keyboard as readily as it happened in real life.

A "formula" for sweeping to the finish

The only remaining hurdle in the Middle Column approach is the ending (a topic we'll consider in greater depth in chapter seventeen—are you beginning to see a theme here?). Merely stopping the story where your chronology stops might not be dramatic or satisfying enough.

One solution is to point from the end of your narrative still further, toward the future. If the gorilla doesn't die naturally soon enough for scientists, might they resort to euthanasia? The back room of the ex-convent harbors a pimento-stuffing machine—even here, can the forces of progress and pimento paste (ugh) be held back forever?

Another option is to embed in the ending a resonance of the lead. Since the Malibu Theater story opened with a celebrity's phone call, it makes a satisfying end for another celebrity (Mel Gibson, at first mistaken for an Australian bricklayer working on the theater owner's home) to call with a plea for his movie.

Whether the ending looks backward or forward, or even introduces some final surprise, the Middle Column delivers readers there as surely as the daily closing bell of the stock exchange. Is it a formula? Sure, in the sense that fermenting a bunch of grape juice is the formula for champagne.

Here's the "formula," stripped to its essentials:

1. Grabber lead, often using contrast or the collision of opposites

2. Hook, setting the specific of the lead in a general context, establishing the basis for the reader's interest, and articulating the angle

3. Background and development of the hook

4. Chronological beginning of the story

5. Chronology up to and through the dramatic lead

6. Completing chronology, weaving in remaining exposition necessary to support the story's premise

7. Dramatically satisfying end.

Compare this structure with the inverted pyramid, the spiral and the hourglass. See how much harder it works at earning and keeping the reader's attention? Every component plays a part in sweeping the reader from first word to final sentence. You grab the reader's attention, show him why the rest of the ride will be worth his time, give him what he needs to know to enjoy the ride, zoom along with nary a jarring break nor chance to wander away, and ultimately tie it all together so the whole is more than the sum of the preceding parts.

That's ultimately the task of structure and form: To make a coherent whole that compels the reader's interest. In the next chapter, we'll look at how the pieces of an article can work together to accomplish that "compel" part of the equation; in the chapter that follows, we'll take apart that goal of a "coherent whole."

Neither is the first thing you'd learn in most journalism courses. But, as we've seen with the inverted pyramid, sometimes things get turned upside-down.

CHAPTER THREE

Flow—The Secrets of Keeping Reader Interest

The inconstant reader

Have you ever watched somebody read something you've written when they didn't know the author was looking on? I'm not talking about handing your latest creation to your mom— she has to at least *pretend* to read it all the way to the end. No, let's say you're seated on a bus and the fellow opposite you pulls a magazine out of his briefcase and flips (oh joyous moment!) to an article you wrote. How quickly that ego-satisfying secret thrill can turn to dismay! Your fellow bus rider studies your article for a moment, then lets his attention wander to the window. Eyes flickering back to the magazine, he turns the page too quickly (the lout!) to have fully appreciated the import of your words. You see him studying a bikini-clad woman adorning an ad on the next page. One last glance at your writing, and then he callously flips forward to give his glancing attention to a different article, or perhaps another bikini.

Seeing your hard work in the hands of what manufacturers call an "end user" can be a humbling experience. An article that took you days, even weeks to research and write gets dismissed with a scan, a look at the pictures, and a flip of the page. *What's wrong with people?*

Yet an appreciation for the tenuousness of the writer's grasp on the reader's attention can also be a good learning experience. What's wrong with people? Just like you, they're buffeted by information, dizzied by high-tech distractions, stressed out by the roller coaster of life in our plugged-in, MTV-ized, cyberspaced society. Readers of an earlier era might have had the downtime to grapple with sleepy leads, tortuous structure and sentences that threaten to collapse under their own weight—but not today. If you expect your writing to be consumed in an atmosphere of Walden Pond-like serenity, by readers with nothing on their minds but the languid beauty of your words, you'd better stick to writing for your mom. That is, if she can find time for you between her job, HBO and her Internet account.

Now more than ever, it's up to the writer to grab readers, hold them for the duration of an article, and leave them feeling good at the end of their reading experience. But rather than moaning about readers' hummingbird-like attention spans, writers ought to be relishing this challenge: Writing that arrests the interest of the busy modern reader is also simply better writing. Cut no slack by readers, today's nonfiction writers are forced to practice their craft at its highest level. In their quest to make a coherent whole that compels even the interest of that distracted bozo on the bus, nonfiction writers walk the razor's edge that leads from craft to art.

Just as when you are doing your very best writing you experience an almost timeless sense of unity with your work—what psychologists who study creativity call "flow"—meeting the challenge of today's inconstant readers requires creating a sense of "flow" in the reading. You want your reader to forget he's on a bus, ignore what's out the window, and be swept along by your article.

As Robert Graves and Alan Hodge once advised (quoted in William Safire and Leonard Safir's *Good Advice on Writing*), "There should be two main objectives in ordinary prose writing: to convey a message and to include in it nothing that will distract the reader's attention or check his habitual pace of reading—he should feel that he is seated at ease in a taxi, not riding a temperamental horse through traffic."

Or, to introduce yet another transportation metaphor into this traffic jam, you want the reader to be like a stick tossed into a swiftly running stream. Even if there are rapids or twists in the water, he should be swept along with no opportunity to climb the bank or lodge in a clump of rocks.

The secret to a smooth and uninterrupted journey downstream, of course, lies in the design of the river. If you want your article to flow irresistibly on, you must first plan the course it will take with the tools of structure and flow.

Four flow-stoppers

At minimum, the fundamentals of flow are a roster of negatives. *Don't* make the reader wade through a weak lead. *Don't* forget to tell why he should care about the information you're trying to impart. *Don't* let him wander astray by confusing the chronology or omitting transitions. *Don't* jumble ideas and images.

These *don't*s all represent reader stopping points, flaws that can interrupt your article's flow and give the reader an excuse to flip the page. Though they sound like a litany of negative thinking, these and other flow killers are worth remembering. By understanding their pitfalls and then turning them on their heads—*do* include the vital "who cares?" hook early in the article, for example—you can plan your article's course for a smooth flow from lead to end.

Let's look quickly at four flow-stoppers and how they can lose readers, so that in subsequent chapters—when we turn these *don't*s to *dos*—you'll see why those *do*s are so important:

1. *Leads that lead nowhere*—If you're interested enough in writing to pick up a book on "Structure and Flow," you surely already know that you need to open an article with a bang, a grabber that will make the reader sit up and take notice. But the problem with many articles is that their bang-up leads don't lead the reader anywhere; they're lone firecrackers instead of fuses that keep going after the initial pop.

Typically, such nowhere leads are tacked onto the top strictly for their sizzle, rather than springing naturally from the focus of the story. They're like the sensational headlines on supermarket tabloids ("Madonna and Elvis Adopt Space Alien!"), which snare the eye but don't have much inside to back them up.

Suppose you're writing an article about how to buy the right athletic shoe. One way to open with a bang would be:

> Buying the wrong athletic shoe could mean having a dose of deadly mercury underfoot. A misstep in the shoe store can put you on the trail to being a walking environmental hazard. . . .

Now, it is true that one brand of shoes used mercury in tiny lights that flashed with the wearer's every step. But the avoidance of mercury poisoning isn't your reader's—or your article's—prime concern in selecting sports footwear. You're not writing an article focused on mercury in shoes, so why lead with it?

The point is not only that such a lead is a cheat (which it is), but that it runs the reader into a dead end. To get from that lead to the real focus of your story, you'd need to come to a complete stop and start the article over again. If you could lop off your lead and still have an article that makes sense, it's a sure sign that it's a flow stopper.

To avoid flow-stopping leads, you have to ask yourself questions like these: What's the story really about? Where do you want to lead the reader? What's the "who cares?" element going to be? In the case of our shoe story, the focus is on the bewildering complexity of selecting sports shoes (and offering solutions to this problem). Here's how I started a story for *TWA Ambassador* magazine that was subheadlined, "A Confused Consumer's Guide to Athletic Shoes":

> It used to be so simple. They were called "sneakers," and you wore them for everything from hopscotch to kick-the-can.
>
> No more. In this age of specialization, the all-purpose sneaker has gone the way of one-squad football. Baseball has the designated hitter, and for almost every sport imaginable, there is now a Designated Shoe. . . .

That's an admittedly modest "bang" for an opening. But it did start a dialogue with the reader, pose the problem I planned to address, and let me take the reader in the right direction. It was no deadly mercury—but neither was it a dead end.

2. *Missing hooks*—We've already seen the importance and utility of the "hook"—that paragraph or section that makes clear to the reader what the rest of the article will deliver, and why the reader should care about this subject. A missing hook is a sure flow stopper. If an article rambles on without a clue as to where it's heading or why anybody should want to go along for the ride, readers will start to fall by the wayside. If you've ever thought, "Get to the point!" you know the perils of forgetting the hook.

Think of the hook, though, not just as an answer to "Who cares?" but as a pivot on which your story turns. The hook takes the momentum established by the lead and pushes it onward into the body of the article. That's why the hook often takes the form of a generalization followed by specific examples (the lead having already presented one such example).

For instance, in another *TWA Ambassador* story, I covered the boomlet in free-enterprise, as opposed to governmental, interest in outer space. I opened with six short paragraphs describing my most intriguing example, then went for the hook: "Almost unnoticed, private enterprise has begun staking a claim to the future of space. . . ." That sentence summarized what my story was about; not so coincidentally, it nearly repeated the subhead that went with the piece, "For Entrepreneurs, the Next Space Age Begins on the Bottom Line."

Next I rattled off three timely examples of entrepreneurs "staking a claim to the future of space." Together, they provided bang-bang-bang proof that this subject was worth reading more about.

The third example, by the way, began to blend into the body of my article. You'd be hard-pressed to point to where the hook ended and the rest of the story began—which of course is exactly the point of *flow*.

3. *Confused chronology*—As we saw in the last chapter, simply telling a story in the order that it happened isn't necessarily the best way to structure an article. But departing from a straightforward, linear time sequence has its perils, too.

One bend in the river of time is usually all that your readers will sit still for. If you make too many twists and turns, so the poor reader has to labor to figure out what happened when and in what order, most will just give up.

Remember our imaginary fire story from the previous chapter? What if, for artistic reasons or simply out of authorial disorganization, we tried to assemble it this way:

4. How the firefighters attacked the fire

1. How the fire started

2. How the alarm was sounded

3. The firefighters responded

6. The damage that was left

7. Reactions of the exhausted firefighters

8. Reactions of the stunned homeowners after the firefighters depart

5. How they finally put out the fire

Would anyone keep reading to the last ember?

While this example may seem extreme, the sins against chronology that make it into print are no less alarming. Next time an article you're reading begins to befuddle you with its chain of events, try sketching the timeline of how it presents the facts—you'll see how confused chronology can kill flow.

4. *Transition gaps*—If confused chronology means not having the pieces of your story in the right order, transition gaps result from failing to link the pieces together. Like the scene in the movie *Speed* in which a bus (back to my bus imagery at last!) zooming down a brand-new freeway suddenly comes upon a 50-foot gap in the road, transition gaps force readers to make an uncomfortable leap. Many of them will just hit the brakes instead.

Transition gaps are the most basic kind of flow stopper. As you construct your article, you need to plan a smooth and logical progression from one thought to the next, one paragraph to the next, one section to another.

The epitome of the transition gap is the *non sequitur*—Latin for a conclusion or inference that doesn't follow from the preceding premises. Consider this admittedly silly example:

1. All men are mortal.
2. Socrates is a man.
3. Therefore, Socrates was a great philosopher.

If your transitions similarly leave the reader going, "Huh?" then you need an infusion of logic and smart structure.

But, like leads, transitions can't just be grafted on from nowhere. If your course is held together with patches applied after the fact, pretty soon readers will feel the bumps. Instead, transitions should emerge naturally from the structure of your story; when the parts of your whole are in a coherent order, linking them seamlessly together takes hardly any work at all.

If you're beginning to think that all these flow stoppers are the fault of sloppy structure, you're getting the idea. Leads that go nowhere, missing hooks, chronological confusion and transitional gaps all are symptoms of structural sickness. The cure is to get your structure right from the start—and then, almost magically, you'll find that most of the challenges of flow have solved themselves. Solid structure gives you flowing leads, natural hooks, clear chronology and ready-made transitions. Get your structure right, and not even that bozo on the bus will be able to turn away from what you have to say.

Figuring out exactly what you have to say, of course, is another challenge—one we'll tackle in the next chapter.

Focus

Reducing before you write

Imagine that you're an astronomer, swinging a great big telescope across the sky. If you've ever peered through even a backyard telescope, you know how quickly—and unsteadily—the stars sweep through your field of view. Bump the telescope and your chosen constellation is lost; breathe too hard and the stars shake before your eyes. It's easy to spend a whole night squinting through a telescope at the immensity overhead and never really *see* anything.

The skilled astronomer, however, knows the secrets of seeing with a telescope, how to use its power to narrow the universe and bring a piece of the heavens down to earth. With practice and training, you too could learn to steady a big telescope and aim it, not just at the stars in general, but at one particular twinkling light. A planet, perhaps. With still more fine-tuning, you could concentrate your view on the features of a planet—Jupiter, let's say—and see clearly enough to learn something from what you see. You could answer, for example, whether the roiling surface of Jupiter still shows any effects from the impact of the comets that struck it so spectacularly in the summer of 1994.

Imagine that you went through all this and on the walk down the hill from the observatory someone asked you, "What did you see?" You would have an answer—one answer, one very specific answer about what happens when a comet meets a giant planet. That's a long way from the amateur's "Oh, I saw some stars."

What the astronomer learns is *focus*. Presented with a whole universe to study, he chooses to focus on some part of it and accomplish something, rather than to merely marvel at the immensity overhead and greet the morning in unaltered ignorance.

And this is likewise the task of the nonfiction writer. When the reader wonders, "What is your article about?" the writer must have an answer—a very specific answer.

The answer comes from focusing in on a particular part of the "sky," from making conscious choices not only about what to write but also about what not to write. As William Zinsser puts it in *On Writing Well,* "Every writing project must be reduced before you start to write it."

You start with the universe. Every story idea can be spun out dozens of ways, just as a telescope can take in any slice of the sky; what makes your story unique is the particular focus, the angle that you take on the subject. "An article is not everything that's true," noted writing expert Gary Provost in *Beyond Style,* "It's every important thing that's true."

Some years ago, for instance, I got an assignment to interview and write a profile of Malcolm Forbes, the colorful founder of the magazine that bears his name. I like to use this assignment as an example because Forbes's life and career were about as big and varied as any galaxy: editor, entrepreneur, author, motorcyclist, collector, balloonist, politician. . . . He brought the notion of "Renaissance man" into the twentieth century. As a result, however, the task of writing a single, 1,500-word article about Malcolm Forbes at first seemed akin to that of an astronomer tackling the Milky Way. I could easily have written 1,500 words just on Forbes's collection of Fabergé eggs.

In fact, that would have made a pretty good magazine article. Why? Because it concentrates on a specific piece of the multifaceted man—in short, it has a focus. The hook of such an article could have gone something like this: "Not only is Malcolm Forbes one of America's best-known magazine editors and a self-proclaimed 'Capitalist Tool,' he is also one of the world's great collectors of one of the world's rarest creations: the Fabergé egg." Such an article wouldn't begin to say "everything that's true" about Malcolm Forbes, Renaissance man, but it *would* manage to say what's important about Malcolm Forbes, Fabergé egg collector. By choosing to leave out 99 percent of what might be said, this approach would make a focused, readable article on the remaining 1 percent.

But that wasn't the focus my editor wanted, and the editor, being the customer in the freelance-writing transaction, is always right. No, the editor wanted an article on Malcolm Forbes as an example of the American Dream in action. You can think of the Fabergé egg article as a very thin slice of the possible Forbes stories, like a geologist picking up one particularly interesting rock from a large site. The American Dream focus was like a geologist taking a core sample: an equally thin slice that cuts through and represents multiple layers of rock. Everything I selected for my article had to support and fit within my focus; anything outside that focus got left in my notebook.

From ideas to angles

The difference between "a profile of Malcolm Forbes" and "a story on how Malcolm Forbes, flamboyant editor and self-proclaimed 'Capitalist Tool' is also the world's leading collector of Fabergé eggs" is the difference between an idea and an angle. You can almost think of it as a mathematical process: "Malcolm Forbes" is an idea; "Malcolm Forbes plus Fabergé eggs" or "Malcolm Forbes divided by the American Dream" are angles.

Ideas, like stars in the night sky, are everywhere. But, as Thomas Mann once observed, "The task of a writer consists in being able to make something out of a idea." That task begins with finding your focus, from which the structure and form of your work must evolve.

In general, the tighter the focus, the better. Zinsser put it bluntly: "Every successful piece of nonfiction should leave the reader with one provocative thought that he or she didn't have before. Not two thoughts, or five—just one."

Let's say you get the idea to write an article about video games. That's an interesting, timely topic, a booming business that affects readers and their kids. But "video games" is an idea, not an article; you need an angle. You could write about how the worlds of video games and Hollywood are intersecting—"video games plus Hollywood," to use our mathematical approach. Or you could write about the battle between Sega and Nintendo for prominence in the industry (and in readers' homes)—"video games divided by power struggle," perhaps. You could even focus on video games that (unlike the ultraviolent games we've heard so much about) actually are educational and good for your kids. To extend the mathematical model to the breaking point, your angle might be expressed as: "video games minus violence plus education equal surprise (good for your kids)."

Because this idea is the most tightly focused, it's probably the one with the most appeal. It also contains an element of surprise, contradicting a commonly held notion ("video games are bad for kids"). Focusing on surprising juxtapositions (video games that are educational, Malcolm Forbes as egg collector) is often a useful way to develop an angle for an article. So if you could come up with a story on "10 Video Games That Are Good for Your Kids" or "Beating Mortal Kombat: Video games that teach your kids positive lessons instead of violence," you'd have a good shot at a sale.

Notice that this angle readily lent itself to being described in a mock headline or subhead. That's a good test for whether you've focused your idea sharply enough: Can you write a headline and subhead that sum up what you're seeking to write about? If not, you probably don't really know what your article is about—you still haven't settled on one tree to climb out of the forest of possibilities.

Six secrets of focus

Let's look at a few real-life examples of magazine articles whose heads and subheads reflect a tight focus:

Here's a story from *Men's Journal* on tennis. Obviously, "tennis" is an idea, not an angle. What about tennis? What's new in tennis? What's the angle? Grass courts. The article reports that grass courts, Wimbledon-style, are growing across the U.S.; since balls "bounce low and fast" on grass, players (readers) need to learn how to handle the action. Think of the focus as "tennis plus grass-courts boom plus adjusting your play." The actual headline and subhead? "Getting Low on Grass: A few tips on sodding the English at their own game."

Or consider a story on parenting advice from *Woman's Day*. Shelves of books have been written on how to be a better parent; to work as a magazine article, the subject has to be sliced as thin as a harried parent's patience. This one took the tack of "Children are extremely sensitive to parents' judgments about them . . ." and focused on the angle of "labeling your children." The headline and subhead perfectly captured the focus: "The Smart One, The Pretty One, The Shy One . . . : Why labeling your children isn't such a good idea."

Finally, a zillion articles have been written lately about the "information superhighway." What focus could make an article on this much-hyped topic stand out? "Battle for the Soul of the Internet" was *Time*'s fresh take: "The world's largest computer network, once the playground of scientists, hackers and gearheads, is being overrun by lawyers, merchants and millions of new users. Is there room for everyone?" Conflict and contrast, as we'll see in the next chapter, are excellent foundations on which to build a story. Here, the *Time* reporter pitted "scientists, hackers and gearheads" against "lawyers, merchants and millions of new users"—and used this conflict between contrasting forces to focus his story.

Good nonfiction stories, like this one, often take the form of a question: "Is there room for everyone?" Whether the question is posed directly or the article assumes the question ("How should you adjust your tennis game for grass courts?" "Why should parents be careful about labeling their children?"), the underlying commitment to coming up with an answer helps focus the writer's mission.

As these examples show, getting from idea to angle, from an expanse of stars to one object smack in focus in your authorial telescope, doesn't have to be hard. Remember these tips for focusing your ideas:

1. *Narrow, narrow, narrow.* Concentrate on a single thought that you want to communicate about your subject.

2. *Combine two ideas and write only about the area where they intersect* (Hollywood and video games, Malcolm Forbes and the American Dream).

3. *Use surprise as a selection tool, focusing only on those elements that will seem fresh or unusual to the reader.*

4. *Test your angle by seeing whether you can write a headline and subhead for it.*

5. *Focus on conflict and contrast.*

6. *Set yourself—and your article—a specific question to answer.* Throw out everything that doesn't help answer the question.

Making your writing go

It's pretty obvious how mastering the art of focusing can help make your writing more interesting to readers—and editors—but what does it have to do with your article's structure and form? Of course, that's what the rest of this book is about. But, for impatient readers, let me spell it out: Like the story itself, your structure must spring from the focus that you select. Focus and form are not merely two elements of writing an article, features that are nice to have, like preferring car mats and a killer stereo when you're shopping for a car. No, they are essential and inseparable, like the engine and the axle—they make your writing go.

Together, your focus and the form that arises from it make a message that is unique to your piece of writing. Think of them like a hologram, the form being the element that lifts the focus from two to three dimensions. Like a hologram, in a successful article the parts are ultimately submerged in the whole. If you cut a piece out of a hologram, the part contains all the essential information of the whole hologram; the hologram has no parts, only wholes.

Tolstoy, who lived before car stereos or holograms, was nonetheless making much the same point when he wrote, "The most important thing in a work of art is that it should have a kind of focus, i.e., there should be some point where all the rays meet or from which they issue. And this focus must not be able to be completely explained in words. This indeed is one of the significant facts about a true work of art— that its content in its entirety can be expressed only by itself."

Let me give you one example of how an article's form springs from its focus, and how the two are inseparably intertwined; we will see many more examples through the rest of this book.

Some years ago, I wrote a profile of Walter Browne, who was then one of the best—but not quite *the* best—chess players in the world. This was not long after Bobby Fischer's triumph in Iceland, and Browne was chasing Fischer to become the *second* American to wear the champion's crown. The similarities between the two men were striking, making more pointed Browne's failure to catch his better-known rival. Now, the other remarkable thing about Walter Browne was that chess was far from the only game he was good at. Poker, backgammon, Scrabble, Ping Pong, you name it and Browne could beat you at it. "I'm the best all-around gamesman in the world," he flatly boasted, and indeed "The Ultimate Gamesman" was the headline of my article.

But there was some irony in that headline, because of course Browne was the embodiment of the cliché, "Jack of all trades, master of none"—at least, not master of the one game, chess, that really mattered to him. This conflict between Browne the ultimate gamesman and Browne the frustrated pursuer of Bobby Fischer, Browne the winner and Browne the loser (at least in relative terms), was the focus of my story.

In a pure example of what we'll later see defined as the "organic" approach to structuring a story (as opposed to the "mechanic" approach), I modeled my article on the alternating moves of a chess game and the alternating squares of a chessboard. Like the back and forth between white and black in a game of chess, my article took turns between the "white," winning and successful side of Walter Browne and the "black," dark and troubled and ultimately unsatisfied side of his life.

I opened with a scene of Browne playing a young opponent at a tournament in Lone Pine, California. It was Browne at his finest ("like playing chess with an oncoming train"), and I used this example of Browne's take-no-prisoners style to explain his success not only at chess but at almost any game he plays: "Walter Browne is a Vince Lombardi dream-come-true: winning, at whatever game, isn't the most important thing—it's the only thing." At the end of the scene, naturally, Browne wins.

But from that triumph I delved into Browne's background, detailing the similarities between his story and Fischer's—and his haunted, unsuccessful pursuit of Fischer. I worked my way toward a quote from Browne's wife, Raquel: "My husband, he needs *peace*."

And so on, back and forth between Browne the ultimate gamesman and Browne the restless man. I alternated between Browne at his finest in the tournament and Browne, after a hard day at the board, strolling through the tiny town and meditating on the modest state of chess as an American sport. Comparable success in football or basketball, after all, would have brought him fame and riches; in chess, he found himself in nowhere places like Lone Pine, where, in the restaurant he frequented, "I've been here three times, and each time the steak has been smaller."

But I left Browne with a "white" move, encountering a chess-playing Russian in the quiet streets of Lone Pine. "At least this is not Russia," his erstwhile opponent reminds him. "This country is *gold*." And I ended:

Browne . . . nods his head and chuckles in the cold mountain night, It's true: in America there are still things to be won. For Walter Browne, for now, that is enough.

I could have written any number of stories about Walter Browne—sharing his successful Scrabble strategies, perhaps, or a first-person, George Plimpton-esque saga of playing against him in various games (and, no doubt, losing). But my particular focus on the dichotomy of his career, once selected, led me to a particular structure for the story. I couldn't have used that structure for any other focus, any more than an astronomer focusing on the Horsehead Nebula could use a map of Jupiter.

There's a saying that "the map is not the destination," but in the successful interweaving of focus and form that rule gets turned on its head. The destination, your focus, leads to the map, your structure, and by the time you get there it's hard to separate one from the other. The place and the plan have merged to become a work of art whose content, in Tolstoy's phrase, "in its entirety can be expressed only by itself."

You are on the observatory hill, the telescope is focused on Jupiter, and you know not only how to see it but how to get there.

CHAPTER FIVE

Conflict and Contrast

Building on the collision of opposites

hat makes a story, any story, grab and hold readers? If you think about the most compelling novels you've read, you're likely to answer: conflict. In fiction, certainly, conflict and contrast, the interaction between two opposing forces, lie at the heart of a story's appeal to readers.

How interesting, after all, would *Moby Dick* have been if Captain Ahab, rather than vowing vengeance after losing his leg to the great white whale, had adopted a policy of live and let live and decided to quit whaling for a life of innkeeping in the New England countryside? That might have been an intriguing *conclusion* to the story—but only if Melville had chosen to first show us the initial battle between Ahab and the whale, the loss of the leg, and Ahab's tortured reaction to his newfound situation (the "backstory," in Hollywood parlance, that happened prior to the opening of the actual novel). Without a dose of conflict, Melville would have had no story to tell—at least not one that anybody would want to read. ("Sorry, Ishmael, you're going to have to find yourself another ship. I'm going to spend the next five hundred pages varnishing my bar and serving ale.")

Indeed, many books of fiction-writing theory and analysis discuss the essential themes of stories in terms of conflict: man vs. nature, man vs. society, man vs. man (typically, too, these books cast their themes in pretty sexist language—my apologies). "Versus" seems to be the most important ingredient in storytelling.

But of course nonfiction is different, isn't it? Unless you happen to be writing about a war or a prizefight, true stories don't lend themselves to the easy "vs." dichotomies of fiction. If you want conflict, go out and find yourself a real-life ship's captain who's lost his leg to a whale; otherwise, you'll have to live without "vs." in your writing, right?

Wrong. Though the conflicts in true stories don't always come with the fireworks allowed in made-up yarns, the collision of opposites still forms the foundation for most reader-grabbing nonfiction.

Consider my Walter Browne profile, described in the previous chapter. A story about a guy who wins at every game he plays would be interesting, but only for awhile. Once the awe wears off (gee, he never loses, huh?), the reader wouldn't have much reason to read on. How will the story come out? Well, the guy will *win*, of course.

What made the Walter Browne story more than a mere curiosity was the conflict between Browne the "ultimate gamesman" and Browne the tortured pursuer of Bobby Fischer. That "vs." gave the story its reader interest—and its shape.

Similarly, suppose you were planning to write a book about the 1927 New York Yankees. Now, a book about baseball's greatest team might be an interesting exercise in nostalgia, but ultimately an account of their inevitable march to the World Series title, setting records en route, would begin to pale unless there were some *downs* to contrast with their *ups*. A book focusing on the turmoil and discord behind the scenes (I'm making this up, of course, and for all I know the 1927 Yankees were a model of harmony) as the team slugged its way into the record books would be far more interesting.

Think of it as the Kryptonite Principle. A story without conflict, in which good effortlessly and invulnerably triumphs over evil, isn't much of a story—whether truth or fiction. That's why Superman's creators had to also create Kryptonite, a force powerful enough to knock their hero off his perch once in awhile. Heroes who never get dirty don't make good reading.

Look for the contrasts

But what does the Kryptonite Principle have to do with the nice little travel story about Paris that you're trying to write? You don't have any heroes or villains, just a perfectly charming "city of light."

Think back on what made good stories—nonfiction stories—in the previous chapter. There weren't many earth-shattering collisions between good and evil, but there were plenty of contrasts: video games with educational value, the way you're used to playing tennis vs. fast and tricky grass courts, parents' tendency to judge kids vs. the unwitting harm those judgments may do, Malcolm Forbes the tough tycoon who collects delicate Fabergé eggs.

If you can't find conflict in your true stories, think contrast—which is essentially "conflict" that may get joined only metaphorically or in the structure of your article, rather than in actual fisticuffs or whale hunting. Does the world really need the umpty-jillionth celebration of "Paris, the city of light?" How about, instead, a story on "Paris underground," taking the city-of-lights, Eiffel Tower image of Paris and contrasting it with the dark mysteries of its catacombs and other underground attractions? (In fact, freelancer Donald Hutera wrote just such a story, and my newspaper's Travel section snapped it up for a lead.)

We're back, of course, to the difference between an idea and an angle. "An article about Paris" is an idea; "Paris underground" is an angle that focuses that idea into a successful article.

Angling your article, in fact, can be thought of as finding a second idea that you can effectively contrast with your primary idea. The interplay between these two contrasts becomes your focus; your structure and form become the strategy by which you bring these contrasting ideas together, oppose them, and finally wrest something larger out of their yin and yang.

When angling your articles, keep in mind the Kryptonite Principle. Remember that Dr. Jekyll wasn't interesting because he was an upstanding man of science; he was worth reading about because he was also Mr. Hyde. Whether fiction or non-, stories about virtuous nuns, the unsullied march of progress, or winners who've never had to overcome adversity don't make compelling reading. Look for the contrasts: the nun who used to be a stripper, the mammoth project for progress that's had some horrible unintended side effect, the baseball pitcher with only one arm.

Take the battle against smallpox, for example. Destroying the last of the smallpox virus is obviously A Good Thing, right? Not so—and *New York Times Magazine* writer Charles Siebert made a fascinating article out of the contrast between the evil of smallpox and the reasons to save the last strains of the virus. "Save Smallpox? Are You Crazy?" was the headline, and the cover copy explained: "The deadly smallpox virus has been eradicated. Its last remains sit in frozen vials five thousand miles apart, awaiting execution. Scientists have twice put off throwing the switch. A furious debate rages. Does the killer have something left to teach us?"

The collision between the scourge of smallpox and its scientific potential gave Siebert his focus, and out of it came the form and structure of his article. He had to recount, on the one hand, the historical ravages of the disease and the decades-long battle to conquer it; on the other hand, his story had to explain the reasons some scientists think smallpox should be saved, and how the virus's genetic secrets might help combat other ills, such as AIDS. *The good side of smallpox?* It's hard to think of a better example of angling an idea.

Adding the unexpected

The collision of opposites underlying your article doesn't have to be as simple as good vs. evil, however. As the smallpox example also suggests, a fascinating story can be built on the contrast between the expected (smallpox is bad; kill it) and the unexpected (smallpox can teach us something; save it).

To see how the addition of the unexpected can shape a story, think back on the examples from *The Wall Street Journal* in chapter two: a little one-screen theater gets pleading phone calls from the likes of Warren Beatty, a modern-day poacher arms himself with a slingshot, vocational students attend a fancy prom. None of these stories would hold much interest with their unexpected elements lopped off: a small theater in Malibu, a poacher, yet another trip to the prom. Ho-hum. They're only ideas, desperately awaiting angles.

Or consider Academy Awards time. Every March we see a zillion stories about the Oscars, predictions of who will win and recollections of past winners. "Winning," in fact, is the essence of Oscar night, so "Oscar winners" is another tautology in need of angling on its head. That's why I wrote a story for *TWA Ambassador* on "Oscar's Losers": the addition of the unexpected element (losing) made for a fresh story worth writing. I covered all the great performers and performances of the past that, in retrospect, you would expect to have won an Oscar—

but they didn't.

Another angle I might have taken on the Academy Awards would be to show how they have changed over the years, how something that was once true has become or is becoming no longer true. Like the contrast between the expected and the unexpected, the collision of old and new can be something to build a story on. Think of *The Wall Street Journal* story in chapter two about the threatened mechanization of pimento stuffing—the old way versus the new. Or, if you were still struggling with that Paris travel story, you might well ask yourself, "What's new about Paris?"

"What's new?" For editors trying to put out timely publications, it's not just a passing pleasantry; it's a thrust to the heart of a proposed article. What's new about this subject? What's different? The answer to those questions can form the essence of your article's hook, telling editors and readers alike why *this* article about pimentos or Paris is different from any previous one they've ever read.

And what if there really isn't anything new or unexpected? That doesn't mean you can't write an article or a must-read-on hook to your story. There are still more subtle contrasts deep within your topic that can be brought out and focused into an article.

Take diamonds. If a diamond is forever, how can there be anything new to write about diamonds? And what could be unexpected or surprising about diamonds? A soft diamond, now that would make a good story, but no such luck in nature. Diamonds don't even *do* anything; they just sit around waiting to be mined, then sit some more in wedding rings.

For an article on diamonds, again for *TWA Ambassador*, I decided to focus on the step in-between the diamond mine and the jewelry store. It's in that transition that the diamond—one of the hardest substances on earth, a substance known for its ability to cut almost anything—is itself cut. The immovable object, if you will, meets the irresistible force. And there is some high-priced tension in this collision: Slip when cutting a diamond and a thing of immense value and beauty is instantly reduced to junk. ("It's a very tense business," I noted in my article. "In the Middle Ages, a diamond-cutter who spoiled a stone lost not just a customer, but his life.")

So my idea about diamonds became focused on the contrast of cutting the hardest substance, on bejeweled success vs. career- (or life-)

threatening failure. "How To Cut a Diamond" was the headline, with the tongue-in-cheek answering subhead, "Very carefully, of course." Since the real answer was obviously a bit more complicated, readers were intrigued.

I opened with the true story of the cutting of a $1.25 million birthday present for King Edward VII in 1907. On the first strike, the blade broke and the assembled royalty gasped. After the second, successful strike, the diamond cutter fainted dead away. My lead, capturing both the hardness of diamonds and the high stakes of cutting them, immediately put my angle into focus.

After putting the intricacies and the history of diamond-cutting under this lens, elaborating on both the special challenge and the risks and rewards, I concluded with one more contrast—this one subtle, mostly a play on words. The business has really changed very little, said one expert I quoted, from those old days described in my lead. "You might even say," I added, "that diamond cutting is forever."

Unlike diamonds, of course, which are valued for their purity, the world that the nonfiction writer chronicles is anything but pure or singular. It's a complex stew of conflict and collision, surprise and change. And the writer seeking to build compelling stories can only say, "Thank goodness."

CHAPTER SIX

Unity

The essence of beauty

As important as conflict and contrast are to a piece of nonfiction, the work also has to hang together as a whole. That is, it has to have *unity*.

Samuel Taylor Coleridge defined this combination of "multeity in unity" as "the essence of beauty." That is, although your writing encompasses a variety of subjects—and, indeed, deliberately pits contrasting and conflicting subjects against one another—the pieces come together as a whole. Nothing jars the reader; no portion of your article seems not to belong. All the elements blend seamlessly (remember the importance of creating reader "flow") to communicate a single idea.

As Gary Provost puts it in *Beyond Style*, "Unity, that quality of oneness in your writing, means that everything you write should look as if it were written at one time, by one person, with one purpose, using one language."

Variety may be the spice of life, but unity is the foundation of an effective piece of writing. "Unity is the anchor of good writing," advises William Zinsser. "It not only keeps the reader from straggling off in all directions; it satisfies the reader's unconscious need for order and gives reassurance that all is well at the helm."

Unity provides evidence that someone is in charge, that there is an authorial maestro (that's you!) ordering the chaos of ordinary life into a purposeful whole. Unity means that every element of an article has a part to play, that no paragraph (not even a sentence!) could be eliminated without losing something of the overall message. If you go back to our notion of a piece of nonfiction as resembling a hologram, then unity is the art of making every piece an indivisible part of the whole: Like a hologram, each part should carry a sense of the whole.

For the reader, unity includes an element of trust: *Trust me*, the author is saying, *this will all come together in the end*. Unity inspires the otherwise impatient reader to stick with apparent detours, confident that they will ultimately return to the main road.

For the nonfiction author, then, unity begins with leaving things out. Remember the idea of focus, from chapter four? Achieving unity in your writing starts with ruthlessly cutting anything that doesn't fit your focus. In *Beyond Style*, Provost advised, "To achieve unity in your writing you must leave out anything that doesn't belong there, no matter how witty, poetic or profound it is. . . . The fact that life just sprawls all over the place is kind of scary, and so human beings look to artists like you and me to organize life, to make sense out of it. . . . Where there is no unity there is no sense of satisfaction."

Unity is, in large part, the business of leaving the reader satisfied. You are asking the reader to come along with you on a journey, and incumbent upon the invitation is the supposition that you, the author, know where we're going. No detours, no false trails are allowed. Even the steps that seem to lead off into the woods must reveal themselves as essential to the journey.

Unity, in short, comes from focus and discipline. It runs through the warp of your article like the woof of a weaving: Miss a thread, and the whole thing might unravel.

Leaving out the "good stuff"

To show how unity starts by leaving things out, let's look at an article I did a few years back for *Savvy* magazine on an entrepreneur named Christina Lawlor. What made Lawlor worth *Savvy*'s notice was that she was a winemaker and that she plied her trade in Iowa, of all places. Iowa and wine—there's your contrast. And there was my focus: How could a "savvy" winemaker/entrepreneur make a go of it in Iowa?

Savvy readers wanted to know the marketing tactics Lawlor used to survive in a business dominated by mega-vintners like the Gallos, firms that use more wine just to fill the hoses between barrel and vat than Lawlor makes in a year. This was a magazine for business women, not *Bon Appetit*.

So I left out a lot of good stuff. My notes ran twenty pages; the finished story, just four. I didn't list her whole line of wines or describe the subtle differences in their tastes. I had some good quotes on how French hybrid grapes, those hardy enough to weather Midwestern winters, compare to their pampered California kin. Ditto with Lawlor on her wines versus Mogen David's. None of that made it into the article, since I was writing about business and marketing, not the niceties of bouquet and fruit.

But I didn't leave out any good stuff about how Lawlor found success on "the boutique level." I honed in on her philosophy: "I realized what it takes to make money in the wine business: a concentrated number of people coming by your door." Lawlor had hit on the notion that visiting a winery—even an Iowa winery—could be an *experience*. I wrote about her tours, her promotional ventures like the hot-air balloon festival and the jazz and bluegrass concerts, her expansion into Ulysses S. Grant's hometown in Illinois—and how she capitalized on Grant's appeal by sticking his face on her labels.

In short, I wrote about what Lawlor had learned that could be applied to any small business. That was my focus; anything that didn't fit never made it out of my notebook. As a result, the reader never stumbled over paragraphs that seemed out of place. The reader trusted me to deliver a lively lesson in overcoming a marketing challenge (sort of the converse of selling refrigerators to Eskimos), and I delivered.

Why not include some fascinating facts about Midwestern grape-growing or some anecdotes about Lawlor's enology training as the first woman to graduate from the University of California-Fresno's wine-making program? "It's not part of what I'm doing," as Provost puts it—another way of saying it would violate the unity of the article. Heck, why not include a brief history of Iowa, a dissertation on corn farming, or a fascinating (to me, anyway) digression on bird species found along the nearby Mississippi River?

Unity, unity, unity. Unity commands, "Leave it out!" And if you can cut it out without hurting your overall message—cut away.

Watch your tone

But unity isn't just a question of content. Readers also expect a *unity of tone.*

To cite an extreme example, if you're writing an article about a family's heroic and tragic efforts to cope with their child's illness, a lapse into puns and wordplay would violate the unity. A skillful writer can successfully blend comedy and tragedy, but only with careful preparation—and as part of a greater tragicomic unity of tone. You can't suddenly veer from Macbeth to Monty Python without violating the reader's trust.

Unity of tone is important not just in the extremes. In my Lawlor article, for instance, I aimed for a certain businesslike breeziness. My opening line was, "When you think of Iowa, you think of corn—not wine," and that signaled the bright, fast-moving style to come. Yet I never descended into guffaws; this was a *business* article. The breezy writing was studded with statistics. Anecdotes were balanced with marketing know-how.

To maintain unity of tone, it helps to keep in mind an imagined audience for your article. Just as your focus determines what you're writing about, your audience determines how you write it. Your tone would be very different for an audience of professional women than for a readership of teenage girls, to cite another extreme example.

If you think of your focus as a highway down which you are leading the reader, then your tone is like the surface of the road. Don't rattle the reader's teeth one minute, then sail smoothly along the next. The reader can get used to an interstate or a gravel road or anything in-between; it's the stretch of gravel smack in the middle of the interstate that's jarring.

Unity of viewpoint and pronoun

To extend this metaphor possibly past the breaking point, it's also not a good idea to suddenly switch drivers. That is, your nonfiction should have a *unity of viewpoint* and, even more basic, a *unity of pronoun.* The two are intertwined but not identical, and volumes have been written on viewpoint, especially in fiction. For our purposes, let's stick to a few essential dos and don'ts.

The viewpoint of my Lawlor profile was pretty simple: I focused on her as a winery entrepreneur. Most of the quotes came from her and most of the information was filtered through her. The reader got the feeling of sitting in Christina Wine Cellars, chatting with the proprietor about what she does, her career thus far, and her hopes for the future. Any comments from other people about Lawlor were presented as asides, filling in any gaps caused by viewing the story through Lawlor's perspective.

Now suppose that instead of a business article I'd been writing a travel piece about wineries in the unlikely locale of the upper Midwest—in fact, I wrote just such an article for *Travel & Leisure*, which also included Lawlor. In the travel version, the viewpoint was that of a tourist accompanied by an invisible author/tour guide. Instead of lingering on Lawlor, my "camera" panned and zoomed through her winery much as a traveler's eye would, showing what the reader would see if following in my footsteps. Because my focus was broader—covering several wineries—I led readers on similar verbal tours of other spots.

If you're beginning to think that questions of unity are interconnected with those of focus, you're right. Both in the big picture (what do I put in? what do I leave out?) and in the details, unity represents the unfolding of your focus through every aspect of an article. The focus largely determines your tone and your viewpoint.

Focus even influences the specific aspect of viewpoint that we're calling unity of pronoun, which is simply whether you're writing in the third person, second person or first person. I list them in that order because that's generally the order of their usefulness to the nonfiction writer. Third person, obviously, means writing about a subject other than the author—in this case, Christina Lawlor. Third person works naturally for profiles and most reported pieces. Second person— "you"—is far more useful in nonfiction than in fiction, where it's mostly the tool of experimental fiction ("You are standing on a ledge . . ."). Second person is essential to service pieces, whether technological ("First you plug in the hard drive . . .") or psychological ("If you sometimes experience depression . . ."). First person—too often the first choice of novice nonfiction writers—works best for personal essays, expert accounts (like this book), and reported pieces that really, truly demand the author's involvement. (Most of these, on critical examination, would work just fine with the "I" excised.)

As you can see, the focus predisposes the choice of pronoun. Once that choice is made, unity demands that you stick with it. Other pronouns may intrude, but the basic pronoun "viewpoint"—who is in the driver's seat—should remain the same from lead to ending. In my Lawlor piece, for example, though I used "you" in the first line, the article was clearly in the third person throughout. A second-person piece often requires some third-person expertise, but that emphasis on "you" must be clear and consistent. And once you've committed to first person, you the author can't suddenly fade into the background.

Beware, too, of violating the unity of pronoun with unexpected and unnecessary detours. If you've written 3,500 words without interjecting "I" into an article, a sudden first-person paragraph will jar the reader. If you haven't already addressed the reader as "you" by the halfway point of an article, an excursion into the second person will seem abrupt. In either case, you're violating the unity of the piece— upsetting the reader's expectations and endangering his trust.

Unifying where and when

Just as the reader expects a unity of *who*, your article creates certain expectations about *where*—a *unity of place*. My Lawlor profile was firmly situated in McGregor, Iowa. Side trips—to expansion wineries in Wisconsin and Illinois—were clearly signalled, and even then it was evident that the "conversation" was taking place in McGregor.

The place of your article can change within a few paragraphs—as when my *Travel & Leisure* story shifted from McGregor to a winery in Minnesota—but the whole focus must change with it. You can't keep one foot in Iowa while you range northward to Minnesota; the reader will get dizzy. So once I'd planted the reader in a Minnesota winery, I couldn't interject some scene or anecdote from back in McGregor without violating the unity of place.

This sounds more complicated than it is. When structuring your nonfiction, just try to answer this question at each point along the way: *Where am I with the reader now?* Or, if you think of your structure as like a screenplay, ask yourself: *Where is my camera at this point?* Your article can't be in two places at once any more than a movie camera can be.

The same goes for time—the *when* of a piece of writing. You can't mix then and now willy-nilly without leaving the confused reader in the dust. At its most basic, this is the *unity of tense*.

Fiction tends to operate in the past tense, as though the author is recounting a story that has happened. Nonfiction, particularly the magazine article, works more naturally in the present tense, which says, *You are there.*

Thus nonfiction can march along quite comfortably with events unfolding seemingly before the reader's eyes: "she says," "she expects," and even "she walks past row upon row of wine casks." The "backstory"—how the present situation came to be—is then readily identified by a switch to the past tense.

Present tense works particularly well for service pieces. If you're writing a problem-solving article, the reader's problem is very much in the present tense—at least until he's tried your solution! Similarly, in a travel article you want to sweep the reader along on an imaginary journey that suggests the ease with which present-tense imagination could become future-tense reality.

Nonetheless, past tense can also work for nonfiction just as for fiction, particularly when an event is clearly over and done with. (A present-tense description of Christmas Day that sees print in February, for example, might seem oddly time-warped.)

Once again, your focus strongly inclines your choice of tense—and once you've made your choice, stick with it. Cruising along in present tense and then slipping into "he said" (except for background or flashback) violates the unity of tense. If you don't know what time it is, how can you expect your reader to keep track—or care?

More broadly, the unity of tense informs a *unity of time*. Chronology aside (that's a later chapter!), your story takes place within a certain swath of time. That might be a generic present day, an unspecified recent past, or a specific chunk of the past. In any case, events that are backstory or flashback clearly take place *before* the time of your story; future possibilities as well as "how it all turned out" epilogues lie *after* your story's time.

My Lawlor profile, for example, was set in a generic *now*. Her enology education and the hard lessons she'd learned about winery marketing were in the past. Her first opportunity to crush her own fruit, at her new Illinois winery, lay in the future. To mix these up without clear chronological signals to the reader would be to invite confusion.

Many of these choices of unities require little conscious reflection; they just come naturally. But it's important to see them all as aspects of your story's focus: What story are you telling? What's the point? What tone does this focus demand? Whose eyes are we seeing through? Where and when is this story happening?

Real life often seems a meaningless and contradictory mess. Your nonfiction, however "real," must be otherwise. It must achieve a unity that satisfies the reader, that cuts through the mess of real life to make meaning and order. Unity in an article is like the difference between sunlight and a laser beam: Sunlight is pleasant enough, but laser light, focused and unified into a single stream of photons, can cut to the quick.

CHAPTER SEVEN

Rhythm

Learning "an ear for the language"

Take the notes of a Beethoven symphony and play them all exactly the same: one quarter-note after another, in a monotonous string of music. Don't vary the tempo from section to section, movement to movement. Just . . . play . . . the . . . notes.

Pretty soon those listening to this little experiment would start wishing *they* were deaf. The notes might be all Beethoven, but without the great composer's rhythms, they might as well be the "music" of a baby banging a spoon on his high-chair tray.

Rhythm—you've gotta have it. Just as rhythm is the difference between a masterwork of music and the listening equivalent of a dental drill, rhythm makes nonfiction sing. Rhythm is the difference between a story that leaves the reader bored or (just as bad) exhausted by its frantic pace, and a piece of writing that, in its artful ebbs and flows, forms a satisfying reading experience. Rhythm—both the larger rhythms of your article's lead, development and climax and the individual rhythms within and between sentences—is as important to your nonfiction as it is to symphonies or sonnets.

"Language is indefinite, formless without rhythm, and what is formless is hard to understand, or to remember," writing teacher Leon Surmelian observed in *Techniques of Fiction Writing: Measure and Mad-*

ness. "Rhythm puts order in the disorder of words, organizes the language, makes it more comprehensible. Rhythm is the heartbeat of prose, as vital, distinct, and mysterious as the rhythm of the body. . . . Rhythm gives prose its breath, its forward movement, its vitality, and is a basic ingredient in all good writing, as it is indeed in all art."

In evaluating writers as an editor and as a boss, I always look first to see whether they have "an ear for the language." Hard to describe, even harder to define, it's one of those "I know it when I see it" (or, in this case, read it) qualities. And in many ways that ineffable "ear for the language" comes down to rhythm.

I look for this musical sense of the English language first, I'll confess, because it seems largely a gift—either you have it or you don't. If you don't have it, I'd rather not have to work with you, because rhythm may be the hardest writing skill to teach.

But before you skip this chapter in disgust *(great, a chapter teaching the unteachable!),* let me quickly add that a sense of the rhythm of writing *can* be nurtured, developed, polished. Let's assume that you have at least a raw "ear for the language"—otherwise you'd probably have given up writing by now in favor of plumbing or nuclear physics—and that our goal in this chapter is to suggest some principles that may help fine-tune it.

Yes, there's hope even for those who might at first beat seem rhythmically impaired. Heck, I'm a lousy dancer and couldn't tell Beethoven from Mozart if my typing finger depended on it. (Yes, I'm one of those unrepentant one-finger typists—but you ought to hear the rhythm I get on my computer keyboard!)

Pacing yourself—and the reader

The overall rhythm of an article is deeply intertwined with the structures you create for each piece of nonfiction. You begin setting the rhythm for the reader with your lead and must maintain and sustain it through your final sentence.

In the largest sense, rhythm is interchangeable with pace. As you pace the unfolding of your story, revealing the facts in dribbles and bursts and orchestrating the drama of events in the telling, you create a rhythm for the reader. You don't save all the good stuff for the end, for instance, because then nobody would read that far. You hold off on the slowest exposition until the reader is well and truly hooked. You pit contrasting ideas against each other, like the "black" and "white" sections of my Walter Browne profile. You build excitement with short bursts of revelation, playing these off against longer, more languid sections.

Just as a movie director arranges his film in scenes—not all the same length, not all the same impact—you arrange your article for maximum effect. The goal of this arrangement, like the pacing of a film, is to draw your audience in, keep them riveted, and leave them with a powerful impact.

Let's look at the "scenes" in a short article I wrote about a Wisconsin farmer who, instead of the usual farm animals such as cows and sheep, raised elk and buffalo. You'll see that the revving and braking rhythms created by the arrangement of scenes give the story a pace that complements the structure of the information.

Thinking like a movie director, I wanted to open with an "establishing shot" that communicated the power and beauty of these animals. (The unusual nature of the animals, after all, formed the focus of my story.) So I began:

> Penned by wooden fences and blue hills bristled with trees, forty buffalo snort steam into the winter air. They pad and shudder like captive locomotives. A big bull lumbers into profile against the silver-bright sky—an old nickel come to life. . . .

A second, similar paragraph described the elk occupying the opposite field. After these two slow, scene-setting paragraphs, I abruptly changed pace:

> Between the buffalo and the elk, Robert S. Johnson is trying to start his truck.

If this opening were reduced to sound effects, it would go like this: *swooosh-swooosh-bang!* The *bang!* was deliberate, and matched to the subject matter. Rhythmically as well as literally, I wanted to set Johnson between and in contrast to the buffalo and the elk. At first glance, Johnson, not the animals, is the one who doesn't seem to fit in this picture—what's this farmer doing in the midst of apparently wild game? The rhythm of the writing reinforced the surprise. (Even the sound of the last word in the sentence—the harsh *truck*—added to the desired *bang!*)

But, having achieved my *bang!*, I didn't want to put the reader off entirely. Now I had to draw the reader into Johnson's world, just as I had painted the picture of the animals. So I quoted him on the dangers of elk ("An elk could kill you," he says, clambering into the cab as forty pairs of eyes study him . . ."), chronicled his actions in and around the truck as he talked, and devoted a paragraph to describing him, much as I had the buffalo and elk.

Having thus balanced the picture, I could then pick up the pace a bit. The paragraphs turned shorter and punchier again, matching the action in the story as the truck, too, revs up and goes through the gate to Johnson's farmhouse:

> "They're fun to raise," he goes on, hopping to the snow. "It's just one of those goals you set when you're young, right or wrong."
>
> It would be easier to get the elk to elaborate. "No more reason. Why do people raise chihuahuas?"

(Note how the rhythm of the mini-scenes that focus most tightly on Johnson mirror his short-spoken style. Try to make your rhythm match your subject—don't write quick, choppy prose about a mighty river or long, slowly paced paragraphs about, well, a chihuahua.)

Once I'd gotten him to his farmhouse, it was time to step back and slow down again for more scene-setting. The scene—rural Wisconsin—was important to the story, because my angle depended on the juxtaposition of elk and buffalo with a scene where you'd expect cows and horses. So, next, three slower paragraphs described the farm and Johnson's background in game farming.

Then I wanted to share some information about the practice and business of game farming. But this wasn't a lecture; I quickened the pace to speed readers painlessly through a flurry of facts.

Finally, I came to a subject that Johnson warmed to ("But ask Johnson about buffalo meat, and he gets going like a carnivorous Euell Gibbons. . . ."), and I let the pace slow down so readers could hear him. Because I had earlier established his laconic response to other topics, the contrasting rhythm here reinforced how at long last "he gets going" on this subject. He "goes on," too, about buffalo hides, and the story matched his pace.

By this point I'd done most of my story's business—set the scene, introduced my subject, explored my angle, delivered the necessary background, taught readers something about game farming (all that most would want to know!). But I couldn't just stop after Johnson's monologue; it would be like pulling the plug without warning. The story had to wind down—or wind back to its beginning—both in subject and in pace.

I began this closing scene with Johnson jumping back onto his truck ("with an animal grace and economy of movement"). That motion signalled a return to the pithy mode in which we met him. A few quick, unsentimental observations about the simplicity of his animals' lives and their potential for mayhem, and then he said to me: "Well, I should let you be going."

With that, I and the reader left Johnson, and the story made one last change of pace. I returned to the rhythms of the lead even as my focus returned to the scene I started with—but with one difference. By the end I'd shown that the plain-spoken Johnson and his animals were not as unlikely a match as the *bang!* of my lead had suggested. In the rhythm of my writing and in my closing viewpoint I brought them together:

> Robert Johnson turns back to his buffalo and his elk. For a moment, he appears as a single figure silhouetted against the low brooding shapes of the animals. Then distance and haze make them all seem as one.

The long and the short of rhythm

These rhythms—the pace of your story—are inseparable from your structure. You can't put the organization of information in one hand and the pace of presenting it in the other, any more than you can separate the notes and the rhythm of a symphony and call either one "music."

It's similarly hard to draw the line between the larger rhythms of your writing and the particular rhythm of sentences and words. Rhythm depends on the relationship between elements: one note following another, one sentence playing off the previous sentence.

Still, we can look at some of the smaller-scale factors that add to the "music" of your writing—while keeping in mind that it's the interplay of all these elements that makes an article into a work of art.

James J. Kilpatrick describes this rhythm of words and sentences as the "cadence" of writing. "By that, I do not mean metronomic regularity," he cautions. "I certainly don't mean that we should strive for a singsong effect; for if you get to be self-conscious, if you strive for rhythm only, you will wind up getting dizzy, you will sound like Hiawatha. . . . No, I suggest only that we cultivate the inner ear. Let us listen to our sentences as they break upon the mind."

For example, just as the paragraphs in my game-farmer story became longer and more leisurely when the subject demanded, so too can individual sentences reflect their substance. Here's how Surmelian puts it: "Good prose, like spoken speech, has plenty of movement in it, its pace determined largely by the action. At a climactic point the language, like the characters, might be a little breathless, the sentences and paragraphs shorter, conjunctions omitted, the dialogue brief, sometimes gasping, staccato. When the tension relaxes, the movement of the prose slows down, the sentences become longer, flowing."

You wouldn't want to write a whole article in an unbroken string of long sentences, any more than you'd write nothing but staccato bursts of short sentences. Either extreme would wear quickly on the reader. Just as important, either extreme would sacrifice the writer's rhythmic tools of variation and contrast.

Consider this paragraph from my game-herding story:

> The wooden sign on the plain white house announces this as "Hardrock Game Farms." The farm stretches about three hundred acres in a hollow in the rolling country between the Wisconsin River and the Mississippi, reached by a succession of back roads guarded by silence and trees. Elk roam roughly one hundred acres, buffalo the rest.

Nothing fancy here, but note how the pace suits the subjects and present the reader with variety: a medium, straightforward sentence for a plain fact; a long, winding sentence about rolling river country; a short sentence made of two succeedingly brief clauses for the facts about the surprising additions to this landscape.

See how much less gets done in the reader's mind when the sentences are all short, of similar rhythm:

The wooden sign on the plain white house announces this as "Hardrock Game Farms." The farm stretches about three hundred acres in a hollow between the Wisconsin River and the Mississippi. This rolling country is reached by a succession of back roads. The roads are guarded by silence and trees. Elk roam roughly one hundred acres. Buffalo roam the rest of the acres.

Or, alternatively, consider how the reader's attention flags while the nuance of rhythm is lost when the sentences take on a Faulknerian lengthiness (Faulkner, being Faulkner, could get away with it; most of us mere mortals at the keyboard can't):

The wooden sign on the plain white house announces this as "Hardrock Game Farms," a farm that stretches about 300 acres in a hollow in the rolling country between the Wisconsin River and the Mississippi, reached by a succession of back roads guarded by silence and trees, where elk roam roughly 100 acres, and buffalo roam the rest.

Whew! Actually, that's just *one* sentence, but you get the idea!

Tools from orators and poets

The best approach, of course, is to play long and short sentences, rambling phrases and punchy clauses, against each other for dramatic effect. Long sentences build tension and momentum, which a skillful writer can release with the pinprick of short sentences. Here's a short, simple example from a lead I wrote for a story about a champion coon-hunting dog—note how the long first sentence sets up the short punch line of a second sentence:

Joker has his own post-office box, his own white pickup truck (the "Jokermobile') and his own brand of doghouses. Joker is a dog.

Just listen to the rhythm of those three string-together clauses and of the short sentence that delivers the expectation-puncturing surprise: *bum-ba-dum, bum-ba-dum, bum-ba-dum—ba-bing!* (Hey, I warned you I was a lousy dancer!)

The juxtaposition of long and short sentences can also build momentum, getting a paragraph going like revving an engine. In a masterful *Sports Illustrated* article on a Native American basketball player, writer Gary Smith got the second section of his story started with four sentences of dramatically increasing length:

> Weeping. Did you hear it? There was weeping in the land that day. Sobs for those missing from that glorious caravan, those decaying in the reservation dust, for Dale Spotted and Star Not Afraid and Darrell Hill and Tim Falls Down, Crow stars of the past dead of cirrhosis and suicide and knife-stabbing and a liquor-fogged car wreck.

Count the words per sentence and see how Smith presses the accelerator: one, four, eight, *forty-seven.*

Smith's passage also illustrates the power of repeating a rhythm in sentences or clauses: "Sobs for those [five words], those [five words], for [four examples, linked by *and*], Crow stars of the past dead of [four causes, linked by *and*]."

More specifically, parallel construction can be a potent rhythmic tool—as skilled orators well know. Look at the speeches of Martin Luther King, Jr.: "*I have a dream* that one day on the red hills of Georgia . . . *I have a dream* that my four little children . . . " "*I refuse to accept* the idea that the 'isness' of man's present nature makes him morally incapable . . . *I refuse to accept* the cynical notion that nation after nation must spiral down a militaristic stairway . . ." Or recall the oratory of President John F. Kennedy: ". . . we shall pay any price, bear any burden, meet any hardship, support any friend, oppose any foe . . ." (verb *any* noun . . .).

Parallel construction can tie one sentence or paragraph to the next, or it can link sections of your story. Such a rhythmic reminder binds the pieces of your article together in the reader's mind. Here's how Gary Smith started the first two parts of his *Sports Illustrated* story:

> Singing. Did you hear it? There was singing in the land once more that day.

> Weeping. Did you hear it? There was weeping in the land that day.

Just as the artful nonfiction writer can borrow from oratory, so too can you learn from poetry. Jon Franklin wrote most of his narrative for the Pulitzer Prize-winning "Mrs. Kelly's Monster," about a brain operation, in blank verse. "Though few readers recognize this fact," Franklin comments in *Writing for Story*, "it has a definite psychological effect that contributes significantly to the overall dramatic nature of the story."

Listen to the rhythms of Franklin's opening paragraph:

> In the cold hours of a winter morning Dr. Thomas Barbee Ducker, chief brain surgeon at the University of Maryland Hospital, rises before dawn. His wife serves him waffles but no coffee. Coffee makes his hands shake.

The story starts with a rush of words that rapidly sets the scene ("In the cold hours of a winter morning Dr. Thomas Barbee Ducker, chief brain surgeon at the University of Maryland Hospital,"), then a brief burst whose rhythm, like its content, signals that something is up ("rises before dawn."). The next sentence, medium-short, sets up the punch at the end of the paragraph, a spare, five-word sentence ("Coffee makes his hands shake."). No word in the entire first paragraph is longer than two syllables unless it has to be ("University," "Maryland"). The effect is like a drumroll before the curtain rises—exactly what Franklin intends to suggest.

Now imagine that same opening with the rhythm stripped away, like the Beethoven symphony with which we started this chapter. The lackluster result might be something like this:

> Dr. Thomas Barbee Ducker, primary neurosurgeon at the University of Maryland Hospital, awakens before dawn. His wife serves him a breakfast of waffles without any coffee. He displays an antipathy to coffee on these pre-surgical mornings because it makes his hands shake.

Does rhythm make a difference in the effectiveness of nonfiction writing? Compare those two versions—you tell me. I'll be over by the stereo, trying to dance the polka to Beethoven's Fifth Symphony. . . .

CHAPTER EIGHT

Structural Choices

The right structural strategy

If you've stuck with me this far, you know that the nonfiction writer's challenge runs something like this: Somehow you need to focus conflict and contrast to achieve unity with a rhythm that's pleasing to readers. Whew! As you might guess from the title of this book, meeting this tall order begins with some hard thinking about structure. In particular, it begins with tough choices about structural strategy.

There's no one right structure for every piece of nonfiction, no single magic answer, but some structural choices do work better for certain articles than others. And just as important as choosing the right structural strategy is understanding the implications of that choice. Remember how Jon Franklin likened the challenge of structure to preparing for a mountain climb, as quoted in chapter one? "Structuring is the art of planning and analysis, of hiring sherpas, accumulating equipment and buying tickets," he said. Making these initial structural choices is like deciding which way you'll choose to get to the top of a mountain: You can do it with a Jeep or you can do it with pitons and ropes. But you can't switch strategies once you're halfway up, and suddenly tossing a rope out your Jeep window or trying to put your pitons into low gear makes no sense.

We've already looked at some of the basic structural choices that a nonfiction writer can make. The much-maligned inverted pyramid is one such choice; the somewhat more flexible hourglass approach is another; the *Wall Street Journal* technique represents another option. We've talked a bit about chronology and the choices that a nonfiction writer must make regarding the ordering of events.

Taking a purely chronological strategy, for example, might mean simply structuring your story in the order in which things happened. Or, delving deeper in search of organizing principles, you might concentrate on the workings of cause and effect on your subject. Here you might mix the strictly chronological ordering of events to better group various causes and their different effects.

We've also looked at the power of conflict and contrast and how the balance of opposing ideas or forces can shape your structure. If your aim is to give both sides of an issue, you might opt for simply presenting one side and then another; in a more sophisticated approach, you could alternate between sides A and B as they look at individual parts of an issue. So your story could take shape this way:

> Sub-issue I
>> A
>> B
> Sub-issue II
>> A
>> B

And so on. This is a popular choice for news-magazine articles and other stories on controversial topics, but it can also be applied to non-news subjects (parents' views on the right age for dating vs. their kids' opinions; buying an IBM-compatible computer vs. buying a Macintosh).

Aside from conflict and contrast, the essence of such a strategy is categorization: You are sorting the information you want to present into two piles. (Of course, you can use more than just two piles.) This categorization principle underlies much of what a nonfiction writer must do (remember the idea of wresting order out of chaos!), but it can also lead to some specific structural choices.

Suppose you're writing an article on what's new in cars this year. You could try to weave all of what's new into one grand concept, but since the reality of your subject is varied and competitive, that's bound to be a stretch. Better to sort what's new into piles and to let those piles form the structural chassis of your story. You could sort by type of vehicle (family sedans, convertibles, light trucks and so forth) or by parts of the car (what's new in sunroofs, stereos, engines, safety gear . . .). Whatever piles you choose, in making the initial choice to compartmentalize and categorize, you've gone a long way toward deciding how to climb that "mountain" of facts.

Stories that take the categorization approach often have a number of subheads or bullet points. Other, similar options might include lists or enumerations ("Ten Tips for Picking the Right Day-Care Center," "The Fifteen Best Places to Spend Your Winter Vacation"). Because such schemes put their structure right on the surface, they aren't particularly subtle or sophisticated—but they are typically easier to write, and often have great reader appeal.

Even more complex pieces of nonfiction, on close examination, may turn out to have a compartmentalization or categorization approach at their center. Heck, take a look at the structure of this book: I chose to organize a wealth of ideas about structure and form in nonfiction under broad categories such as "unity," "transitions" and "endings." Once I made the choices about which categories I would use, I'd made a major stride toward wresting order out of the chaos of possibilities. I was hardly at the mountaintop, but at least I'd laid out my gear.

Organic vs. mechanic structure

If you think about the various structural choices that confront a nonfiction writer, they all fall into two basic kinds of strategies (here we go with categorization again!): Either your structure can grow naturally out of your subject matter or you can, in the act of focusing your idea, impose a structure on the material. That's the difference between (in Samuel Taylor Coleridge's terms) "organic" and "mechanic" structure.

Simple chronological structures, for example, could be categorized as "organic"—because the structure unfolds pretty much like the subject. (It's possible, however, as we'll see, to take a "mechanic" approach to chronology and order events in a way that makes a point you want to make.) Most categorization approaches, on the other hand, are mechanic in nature because they involve the author imposing an order on the subject. (If the order is alphabetical or geographical—north to south, downtown to suburbs—then we're getting into organic territory again. As we'll see, Coleridge's distinction turns out to be more a matter of grays than black-and-white.)

Both methods demand order; the key difference is the source of the organizing principle—whether it springs from within the subject or comes from some idea of the author's.

I like to use several books by John McPhee (all of which began as articles for the *New Yorker*) to illustrate the difference between the organic and mechanic approaches. In McPhee's book *Oranges*, for example, he structures the story around the life cycle of the fruit. *Levels of the Game*, in which McPhee profiled tennis great Arthur Ashe, takes the back-and-forth form of a tennis match. And in perhaps his ultimate tour de force of organic structure, McPhee's *The Search for Marvin Gardens* uses an imaginary Monopoly game to tell the story of Atlantic City. Why is this organic (springing out of the subject) rather than, as it might seem, mechanic (a clever notion of the writer's, laid like a framework upon the subject)? Atlantic City, with its Boardwalk and Atlantic Avenue, was the model for the properties on the Monopoly board. The contrast between the make-believe perfection of the cardboard Monopoly world and the run-down real life of Atlantic City, Monopoly's inspiration, gives the story a power and resonance McPhee couldn't have achieved with any other structure.

Yet for all McPhee's skill and grace with organic structures, as William L. Howarth notes in the introduction to *The John McPhee Reader*, "he has a certain preference for mechanic form, since it arises from human logic." Thus McPhee's *Encounters with the Archdruid*, a profile of Sierra Club president (and "archdruid" environmentalist) David Brower, was "planned *a priori*, as a matrix into which he poured the molten confrontations of Brower and company," Howarth notes. The matrix that McPhee created is diagrammed on the cover of the book: three triangles in a row above a line, below which stands a lone, centered triangle that seems to act as a fulcrum. The three upper triangles represent three environmental antagonists that McPhee planned in advance to pit Brower against. He set Brower (the fulcrum triangle) against a mining proponent, a resort-development booster, and an advocate of a dam project, each at the scene of their conflict. These three "encounters with the archdruid" form the three-part structure of the book.

McPhee also shows the power of manipulating chronology, so that rather than following the straight organic flow of events an article takes a mechanic path defined by the author. Howarth observes, "In recounting Thomas Hoving's discovery of an ivory cross [in *A Roomful of Hovings*], McPhee cuts and reshapes time as though he, too, were a carver in ivory." (As Howarth adds elsewhere in his introduction, "Writers have infinite options for order, and McPhee delights in playing any that do not violate his story's 'logic.' ")

Finally, sometimes a writer starts with an organic approach—a basic chronology, for example—and manipulates it in a mechanical way to make his point, only to wind up back with a form that seems utterly one with the subject matter. In *The Deltoid Pumpkin Seed*, McPhee's account of an experimental hybrid airship/airplane, he deliberately and repeatedly digresses from the straightforward unfolding of events. It's a mechanical strategy, the author commanding control of his story. Yet it creates an organic effect: The lurching back and forth ultimately comes to resemble the fits-and-starts progress of the experiment McPhee is chronicling.

The important thing isn't whether your structure is organic or mechanic—or something of both—but that you think about these choices as you make them. A story about baseball need not take the form of nine parts, or innings, but give it some thought: That's exactly the structure documentary film-maker Ken Burns selected for his mammoth series, *Baseball*. A narrative doesn't have to unfold in the exact order in which it happened; it can follow some other scheme that better fits your focus. On the other hand, the force of what-happened-next? can be mighty compelling.

The key is to have a reason for the structural choices you make. Don't take a Jeep up to the mountaintop just because you're afraid of falling if you take the sheer route. Do it because that's the most scenic way to where you want to go, or because it resonates most powerfully with your idea of a mountain. Maybe it's best to follow the way the mountain wants you to go—the organic approach—but don't reject out of hand the option of blasting your way through the rock.

Structural possibilities: A tough nut to crack

Let's look at some of the structural possibilities for an actual article— a story I wrote about growing pecans in Iowa, far north of the warm southern realms where you'd expect to find pecans—to see how these choices get made. It was a pretty simple story, but frankly I remember it vividly because I had to trek along with these pecan fanatics, through swamps and back country, in search of the elusive northern pecan.

That was the focus of my story, in fact: "Pecan hunters search for a taste of the South way up north" was the headline. My angle was the contrast between pecans, that delectable nut of the balmy South, and the chilly clime of rural Iowa, 380 miles south of the Canadian border. ("Before you laugh, thinking pecans belong next to southern verandas as shade for the quaffing of mint juleps . . ." was how I introduced my, er, nut graf.)

Faced with this raw material and a notebook full of information about nuts, climate and getting my boots all muddy, I might have gone for an all-out organic approach. Without being too precious— the article equivalent of a shape poem—I could have structured the article like a pecan: Extremely hard on the outside (like the likelihood of finding a pecan tree growing wild in Iowa), with two tender halves inside once you finally break through (indeed, I had two protagonists, twin pecan hunters). I suppose I could also have structured the story like a tree: first the roots (a thicket of introductory facts necessary to explain the subject of northern pecans), then a long straight stretch of trunk (the narrative of our search), followed by another branching and finally the "fruit" of the search.

Sticking with the organic principle, I could also have rejected all the forms that reflect the object of the search and concentrated on the quest itself. I could have let the chronology unfold naturally, beginning perhaps with the first of my protagonists getting the crazy notion of looking for pecans in Iowa. Next, not unlike Don Quixote recruiting Sancho Panza, he sells this impossible dream to a partner and off they go. The part of the story that I saw firsthand—slogging through the mud, our pecan hunters already with their quest in mind—would begin maybe halfway through the article.

On the other hand, with my angle firmly in mind, I could have mechanically organized the story in a kind of point-counterpoint scheme: Why pecans won't grow this far north/why they just might after all. Or I could have alternated between facts on northern pecans and facts on their pampered southern kin.

Since I was an actor in this little drama, I could also have used my experiences and reactions to shape the story; being mine, these elements would lend themselves more readily to whatever mechanic scheme I might cook up. Seen through my prism, the small drama of hunting for Iowa pecans could stand for any larger drama that I chose—perhaps some personal crisis or epiphany that I found reflected out among the pecan trees.

A route to a punch line

The actual structure that I selected, not surprisingly, is not quite so neatly categorized. But it's probably best thought of as a mechanic choice, since I played with the order in which I revealed events, the positioning of my "backstory," the point at which I began the narrative, and the way I ended it in order to achieve a desired effect. The effect of this simple little article can be likened, in fact, to the punch line of a joke. And the structure I imposed on my raw material resembled the lead-up to a punch line.

This joke/punch line structure worked because it suited my focus: "Pecan hunters search for a taste of the South way up north." Remember that I even set up the idea of a joke in my hook, with "Before you laugh. . . ." Later, too, I reinforced it with, "Again, stifle that laughter. . . . " And I had one of my protagonists "whooping with laughter" at a yarn his buddy told as we trudged through the backcountry. These guys didn't take this quest too seriously.

In fact, the unspoken (until the end) second half of my focus was that you'd have to be a little bit crazy to go pecan hunting in Iowa. That's the "punch line," if you will, that my whole structure set up. As I described it in my next-to-last paragraph:

> Bill Totten, arm distended by half a pole pruner and legs calf-deep in mucky water, says cheerfully, "You don't have to be crazy to do this—but it helps."

When I spotted that quote in my notes, the whole story came together. I knew at once that my aim would be to lead up to that finish.

So how did I structure my story to get there? The important elements were the search (muddy, middle of nowhere, have to be crazy to do this) and the incongruity of the object of the search (pecans up north).

I started with the search, because that had action and the potential for some colorful description and because I knew I wanted to end, full circle, with a scene from the search:

Mud grabs the bouncing gray Lynx and strands it with a single squish. Tires spin and spew brown clouds, in vain. Let's park here.

I opted *not* to start the chronology with the inception of my protagonists' quixotic goal, back home where they were dry and warm, but with the muddy consequences. I could also have started later, out of the car and well into the back country, but the image of the car stuck in the mud seemed a vivid spot to begin illustrating how you'd have to be crazy to do this. It also let me introduce the information, as one protagonist hops out, undaunted, that he'd worked till two in the morning the night before, only to get up early and drive a couple hours to get here. Crazy, huh?

After setting the muddy scene for three paragraphs, I introduced the object of their quest and, via my hook, element number two: "Most people wouldn't consider growing pecans this far north . . ." *Most* people indeed!

I continued the back and forth between my two key elements through most of the story. They unload their gear (awkward to carry). They taste a few (tiny) northern pecans they'd brought along, "like bloodhounds sniffing a scrap of clothing from the prey." I doled out more details about pecan biology in-between scenes of my pecan hunters getting lost and descending "into black water and brambles."

Finally (and here the chronology is exactly as you'd expect in a straight organic form), our heroes find a bona fide pecan tree. They mark and measure it and snip off graftwood for a university breeding experiment. And then came the quote I'd been building up to: "You don't have to be crazy . . ."

Because I'd set it up, because I'd made the structural choices necessary to get here with the right elements uppermost in the reader's mind, the quote worked much like the punch line of a joke. And so did my rim-shot final, punny paragraph:

Don't say "crazy." Say "nuts."

The quote and my quick comment put into words what the reader had been carefully led to think: These people are nuts to go through all that for such unlikely quarry—nuts, but in an amiable, well-intentioned sort of way.

And of course that's where I left the readers, not with the muddy walk back or the shoving to free the car or the drive home. Never explain a joke or ramble on after the punch line!

We'd come to the mountaintop (however modest the mountain) together, the readers and I. I'd shown them the view I wanted them to see, and it made a particular impression because of the route I'd chosen to get here.

CHAPTER NINE

Outlining

Writing it down

After all this admittedly highfalutin talk about flow and focus and rhythm, it's time to get down to the nuts and bolts and reveal the secret of how to take all these principles and put them into action: outlining. Yes, the most useful tool in the lofty art of writing nonfiction is the lowly craft of putting down on paper what you're going to do before you do it.

Writers may run screaming from the idea, haunted by unhappy grade-school memories, or disdain outlining as inimical to letting their creative juices flow. But if you've been following along so far, you'll see that the hard truth is inescapable: Success with structure and flow depends on finding your focus, selecting an angle, and then harnessing all the material at hand toward that end. To wrest order out of chaos, you must have a plan—a map that gets your story (and the reader) from start to finish. And, whether it's a high-tech creation on a computer complete with Harvard labels and a detailed hierarchy of fonts and indentations or a humble scrawl on a yellow legal pad, the outline is the cartographic key to nonfiction writing.

Rail all you want. Rant about how Mrs. Quimby in the fifth grade drove you crazy with outlines. Go on and on about getting in touch with your muse and wanting to be unfettered by constraints on your inspiration. Once you've got all that out of your system, sit down and start outlining.

Listen to Pulitzer Prize-winner Jon Franklin, in *Writing for Story*: "I don't care what you've heard, or what your literature teacher said, *or even what the writers themselves said*. Every writer of any merit at all during the last 500 years of English history outlined virtually everything he wrote."

Got that? OK. Now, on the other hand, if your objection isn't that you shouldn't or don't want to outline but that you *can't*—that, gosh, it's a fine idea but your head just doesn't work that way—go back and re-read the first eight chapters of this book. Go on, we'll wait.

Back already? Great. By now you should understand that outlining isn't some gimmick, some process external to and imposed upon your nonfiction writing, but an inevitable outgrowth of coming to grips with your story. Focus, angle, rhythm, conflict and contrast, unity, all these elements of a successful article are like the diverse components that make up a symphony. No symphony goes from the composer's head through the musicians to the ears of the audience without a score—which means *writing it down*. Outlining means simply taking all the aspects of a story that you must juggle and *writing them down*.

Franklin is still more blunt in defining a professed inability to outline. "In telling yourself you can't outline, what you're *really* saying is that you can't think your story through," he says in *Writing for Story*, "and if that's actually the case—which I seriously doubt—then you'd better give up your writing ambitions before you become successful enough for people to discover that you don't know what you're talking about."

Of course, if you've stuck with me this far then you know it's not as difficult as it seems to think your story through. And the thinking, not the outlining, is the hardest part.

One method for outlining and order

Whenever I preach the gospel of outlining, I like to use the example of John McPhee, the *New Yorker* writer—not because his approach is the only way or even the best way, but because McPhee's methodical method shows so clearly the connection between the principles of structure and form and the mechanics of outlining.

Not surprisingly, McPhee credits an English teacher, Mrs. Olive McKee, for inspiring his approach to outlining. He defines his outlines as "logical," a term Mrs. McKee would no doubt approve of. Yet McPhee's outlines for his deftly crafted, intricately structured nonfiction tales are no schoolbook I-II-III, A-B-C creation.

As William L. Howarth describes the process in his introduction to *The John McPhee Reader*, McPhee begins by typing up his notes. The typed notes go into a binder. McPhee then works his way through the binder, coding each segment of notes with the topic under which it falls: "Voyageurs" or "Loons," or acronyms such as "GLAT." The topics also go onto index cards, one topic per card.

"After assembling a stack," writes Howarth, "he fans them out and begins to play a sort of writer's solitaire, studying the possibilities of order. Decisions don't come easily; a story has many potential sequences, and each chain produces a calculus of desired and undesired effects. . . ."

When the shuffling of the index cards finally results in a satisfactory structure, McPhee thumbtacks them to a bulletin board. He then photocopies his notes and scissors apart one copy in order to sort the segments of notes, by topic, into file folders. Each folder corresponds to an index card on the bulletin board.

One folder at a time, McPhee writes his way through this "outline." A steel dart on the bulletin board marks his progress through the topics on the index cards.

"Structural order is not just a means of self-discipline for McPhee the writer," Howarth adds. "It is the main ingredient in his work that attracts his reader. Order establishes where the writer and reader are going and when they will arrive at a final destination. . . . McPhee is a craftsman; he understands that his work must always have inherent form."

As you see, McPhee's outline emerges from this inherent form and structural order; the outline and the ordering of the story are indivisible. Methodical, even plodding though his technique may seem, its very mechanical nature forces McPhee to confront the structural challenges of his story—*before* the first draft gets written, not after his story has driven itself off an organizational cliff. The method is mechanical, yes, but the mechanics disguise great artistry: In shuffling his simple index cards, McPhee is like a maestro bringing music out of the multiple voices of the orchestra, or like a sculptor finding the beauty that lies hidden within the stone. This is the deepest work of a nonfiction writer, the architectonics at the heart of every successful article.

A legal-pad blueprint for articles

If you're now running out to buy index cards, file folders and a steel dart, great, you've found the religion of outlining. Your own outlining process doesn't have to be the same as McPhee's, however, or even as complex or as orderly. The secret isn't in the cards, folders and dart but in the organizational thinking that an outline forces you to do.

My own approach to outlining was admittedly inspired by McPhee's, but since most of my nonfiction undertakings are less daunting than his booklength projects, I scaled his process back a bit. (I also honed this technique as a newspaper feature columnist, banging out first three and then four pieces a week, which didn't give me much time for photocopying and scissoring.)

For an article-length project, I start by scratching out my main points, in rough order, on a yellow legal pad. (These are more or less the equivalent of McPhee's index-card topics.) By and large, these points come from my head rather than from my notes. They are subject to change, reordering, addition and deletion. But I figure that if I can't remember a key point without referring to my notes, the point probably won't be memorable to the reader, either.

At this stage I concentrate on the broad motions of the article: where I'll start, what my hook will be, what I need to get done between there and the ending. Relying on my head rather than my notes lets me concentrate on the focus and angle I've chosen, without being tempted by colorful but irrelevant detours from my notebook. Beginning with a pretty skeletal outline keeps my attention on the underlying architectonics—the map from here to there, not the roadside attractions.

Once I've grappled with my basic structural challenges (the legal-pad equivalent of McPhee's index-card shuffling), in a sense my hardest work is done. The rest is filling in the blanks, matching my notes to my outline and fine-tuning.

Next I number the pages of my notebook and go through each page to find material that supports each of the points in my outline. Whenever I find a quote or fact or detail that I'll probably want to use, I highlight it in my notebook and note the page number in my outline. I may also add subpoints to my outline to reflect the details from my notebook. The order of these subpoints, too, is important, and so the outline evolves as it is fleshed out. Here I may even decide which quotes, for example, to use in what order—as indicated by the little page numbers on my legal pad.

After I've worked my way through my notes, I'll quickly review the beefed-up outline to make sure that everything still fits where it is and that the logical flow makes sense. I may move subpoints or whole chunks of outline and attached page notations. The point of outlining isn't to fix your organizational scheme in concrete; rather, it is to force you to confront exactly these structural questions.

The resulting stew of scribbles may look like chaos, but to the writer who has worked it through, this outline is just the opposite: a finely tuned blueprint from which to write. Map in hand, I know where I'm starting, where I'm going and how to get there. Paradoxically liberated by this act of rounding up my thoughts, I am free to concentrate on getting there in style.

Making outlining work for you

How can you best make outlining work for you? Obviously, you need to adapt this philosophy to your own writing style: You might be a scribbler, or you might be a high-tech outliner armed with every computer bell and whistle, or you might be a model outliner who's mastered I-A-1-a style and who isn't about to forget it. The important thing is not how you outline or what color pens you use, but that you make a commitment to grappling with the questions of structure and form before you sit down to write a first draft.

More broadly, making outlining work for you is what the rest of this book is about. (You outline-phobics come back here right now! I promise that this won't remind you of fifth grade in the slightest!) You'll notice that this chapter is the most example-free in the book. That's because so many of the examples we've already seen and most of the examples that lie ahead are built upon a foundation of outlining. To pile on the examples here seemed like overkill!

You can think of all of what has gone before in this book—flow, focus, conflict and contrast, unity, rhythm, your fundamental structural choices—as the challenges that outlining will help you to master in every piece of nonfiction you write. These are the various factors competing for your attention, the elements you must juggle as you pull your story together. Maybe you can keep all these straight in your head—but if your brain works that well maybe you should be applying it to something *really* important, like finding a cure for the common cold or opening childproof caps. Me, I need to write things down to keep them straight; that's why I outline.

The chapters that lie ahead in the next section cover the nuts-and-bolts pieces that make up your outline. As you link these pieces together in your outline, keep in mind all the elements involved in wresting order out of chaos in the creation of nonfiction: focus, unity, rhythm and so on. Each of these elements will affect your choices— what pieces you pick, how you put them in order, how you connect them.

Your tool for bringing together the complex elements of nonfiction with the basic pieces of every story—the lead, chronology, exposition, the ending and so forth—is of course the humble outline. Think of the multiple levels that a John McPhee must work within as he shuffles his index cards: How do his choices affect the overall rhythm of the story? Will this grab the reader's attention as a lead? If that's the lead, what are the implications for the narrative's chronology? How does the lead relate to the ending, and how will the conflicts set up in the "hook" be resolved? The structuring of a nonfiction story resembles a game of three-dimensional chess, with every move rippling not only across the flat horizon of here-to-there but up and down through the story's nuances as well. Index cards or legal pad, computer program or blackboard, however you plan your strategy, the most important thing is that you plan it.

As Jon Franklin puts it, "The truth is that writing is a very complex undertaking, analogous to conducting a military campaign. Things won't simply fall into place because God is on your side. You have to plan for them, and there are far, far too many factors for you to keep them all straight without writing them down."

So if you're ready to do battle, armed with an outline, turn the page and let's meet some of your troops.

Part Two

THE PIECES

CHAPTER TEN

Leads

Avoiding the tailfin lead

Whole books have been written on the mystery and challenge of the lead. Writers agonize over the lead, staring at the blank page or the empty screen until it seems more likely that their eyeballs will pop than that one blessed word will appear to start their story. Editors work their blue pencils to a nub and wear the finish off their "Delete" keys, trying to get the lead right when they think a writer's gotten it wrong.

And no wonder. If an article doesn't start with a bang, the odds of it keeping busy readers much past the first few paragraphs are slim. As William Zinsser puts it bluntly in *On Writing Well*, "The most important sentence in any article is the first one. If it doesn't induce the reader to proceed to the second sentence, your article is dead. And if the second sentence doesn't induce him to continue to the third sentence, it's equally dead"—and so on.

Faced with this weighty opening responsibility, it's not surprising that so many writers freeze up—and that so many others reach into a bag of shopworn tricks that leave them, at lead's end, way out on a limb that's barely attached to the trunk of their article. Gimmick leads, juiced-up leads, falsely mysterious leads—writers, in their desperation to get the darned thing started, have tried just about everything that can be done with a pile of words and some punctuation.

You've seen leads like this (maybe you've even written some):

The false surprise:

Aliens have invaded California! Like a scene straight out of "The War of the Worlds," these aliens are everywhere—in offices, in stores, even in our homes.

But these aliens aren't from Mars. They're illegal aliens, undocumented workers who. . . .

The unwelcome second person:

You are dead. Sixty seconds ago, you were alive, driving your car, heading home from a party. You'd had a little too much to drink.

Every year, drunken driving causes thousands of deaths like yours on U.S. highways. . . .

The Andy Rooney wannabe:

Did you ever wonder how much helium is stored in the U.S. Helium Reserve system? And did you ever wonder how come all that helium doesn't just float off into space?

Answers to those questions and many more can be found in the offices of the American Helium Council. . . .

Aside from being simply awful leads, these made-up examples and their real-life kin commit a structural sin: They are all tacked-on gimmicks, the article equivalents of the humongous tailfins that sprouted on American cars in the Fifties. Did the tailfins make the cars drive better or more smoothly? Did they have anything at all to do with transportation? Nope—they existed solely to catch your eye. From a transportation standpoint, the tailfins might as well have been attached to rocks.

You know by now that we're not looking for leads like tailfins. Rather, a successful lead must be an integral part of the article's overall structure and form. The lead does not stand apart from the whole, a pretty bauble that serves only to entice the unwary reader; it is essential to the whole, the beginning of a journey that you and the reader are taking together.

In particular, the lead must spring from your story's focus and draw the reader effortlessly into your story's core. To continue the automobile analogy, instead of acting as a tailfin, your lead ought to be the spark plug that sets the whole thing in motion.

If that all sounds harder than starting with whatever cute phrase lets you conquer the blank page, it is—unless, of course, you've done your advance work and honed your focus and developed your outline. Then the hard work is done; your lead will practically demand to be written.

And, once written, your lead will lead you seamlessly into the rest of your first draft. You'll be in the driver's seat, not hanging on to the tailfins.

Focusing your lead

The simplest form of a lead that springs from your focus is the lead that just wades right into the heart of your story. It's almost as though you're starting with the nut graf or hook, phrased in a way that immediately engages the reader's interest or empathy. Two or three warm-up sentences and then *bam!* your focus is at the front and center of your story.

That's the approach I took for an assignment for *Logic*, a magazine for Control Data Corp. Here's how the editor summarized my focus in the published article's subhead: "Faced with a predicted shortage of technical brainpower, corporations team up with educators to train the engineers of tomorrow." That meant my article had to accomplish four things:

1. Establish the problem (predicted shortage of technical brainpower)
2. Establish the needs of corporations
3. Establish the needs of colleges and universities
4. Show how those needs have led to corporations teaming up with educators, and how these partnerships have addressed the problem in point 1

A tall order, especially since the editor wanted me to spend the bulk of my word allotment on the specific examples in point 4. So I decided to lead with point 1:

"What do you want to be when you grow up?" Ask any classroom of children that eternal question and the answers will range from "firefighter" to "astronaut" to "cowhand." How many want to be *engineers*? Not a hand will go up. Engineering is hard, complicated and difficult to define with a drama that matches dousing fires or riding the range.

In the United States, companies are realizing . . .

And I was already into point 2. Examples and statistics as I detailed points 2 and 3 would substantiate my lead's broad assertion, but I'd at least gotten the problem on the table and started down the road toward solutions.

Notice, though, that I still sugarcoated the opening. I started with children, a familiar situation, an easy rapport with readers. Not until the third sentence did I mention the hard, complicated and undramatic subject of engineering. You don't need "tailfins," but neither do you want to run the reader down with the first sentence:

Nobody wants to be an engineer. . . .

"Neither do I," thinks the reader, turning the page.

Still, however true to my focus, was this the best possible way for me to start the story? Let's just say it was my best choice given the material I had. If I'd had a real-life anecdote that dramatized the problem, that might have been a more vivid start:

Ten years ago, Professor Charles Smith's Introduction to Engineering class was held in an auditorium seating 200 students. Smith needed a microphone to be heard over the rustle of note-taking. Late-arriving students had to perch on the stairs.

This semester, however, Smith is holding Introduction to Engineering in his office. All three future engineers can fit comfortably around his kitchen-sized conference table. . . .

Another attractive option would have been to depict a scene that exemplified the solution to the problem in action:

The freshmen shoulder their bookbags, flirt and jostle in the hallways just like any other group of college students. But these young engineering students aren't heading to a conventional classroom behind ivied walls. Their classroom is the roaring, clanking heart of a General Motors assembly line. . . .

The important thing to note in these options, like the lead I actually used, is that all spring from the story's focus. They dramatize or otherwise try to intrigue the reader with one of my central points. (After all, it's hard enough to communicate three or four key points, without wasting the lead on making a point not crucial to your article!) All are integral to the thrust of the article—they all do some of the work that my words had to complete. Not a tailfin in the bunch.

Leads from contrast and conflict

Another thing you might have already noticed about these examples, real and fictional, is how heavily they rely on the topic of chapter five: conflict and contrast. Building leads from within your focus, rather than tacking them on as mere adornment, gives you access to the other essential elements of your article—like conflict and contrast.

In my actual lead, the contrast is between kids' traditional ideas about careers and the demanding yet in-demand field of engineering. My made-up "Professor Smith" lead contrasts the popularity of the class a decade ago with today; the scene of students at GM plays stereotypical ideas about college life against the image of a factory.

Because conflict and contrast lie at the heart of so many stories, and because they make for instant reader interest, they are ideal for structuring leads. Conflict and contrast in the lead put the action out front: *Hey, readers, we're butting heads here! Ideas in collision, read all about it!* (Much more interesting and reader-grabbing than harmony, the status quo, or when all is as expected.)

Effective leads pack surprise. They run contrary to expectations or stereotypes. They paint a picture of intellectual gladiators, of an emperor with no clothes, of Christians taking the lions by surprise.

And this only makes sense. Why should the reader read on to learn what he already knows? Who needs to waste time with an article confirming one's expectations? The lure of nonfiction is that you might learn something—and the more surprising the something, the better.

Conflict and contrast lie at the heart of most good profiles, for example. If you went to all the trouble of profiling somebody and didn't learn anything new, why bother to write an article? If you did uncover some surprise or insight, don't hide it—make it the focus of your article and the seed for your lead.

I once set out to do a story on the head of the local IRS office, timed to tax day, April 15. What I found out, however, was that the IRS boss was perhaps the only guy in town who *wasn't* scrambling over taxes on April 15. I harnessed that contrast—the relaxed tax man on the busiest tax day—for my lead:

> Today, tax day, is a day like any other day for Bob Huss, tax man. While his fellow citizens ponder a midnight deadline, the arcane numerology of tax forms and the prospect of Leavenworth, Huss goes about the business of the Internal Revenue Service. Just another working day. . . .

This theme of confounding expectations, set up in the lead, continued through the article. You'd expect a guy who audits your taxes to look scary, right? But Huss proved as ordinary and mild-mannered as they come. And so on. I'd expected April 15 to represent the unleashing of an audit monster; instead, I found an ordinary guy with a job to do.

Similarly, when I went to profile sports tycoon John W. Galbreath, I (and the reader) expected a Donald Trump of the horsey set. What I found instead was a man who could have been anybody's grandpa. So I led with this contrast:

> John W. Galbreath has sold 30,000 homes and changed skylines all over America. His baseball teams have won three World Series. He is the only horse owner to win both the Kentucky Derby (twice) and the English Derby. . . . [His houseguests] include former president Gerald Ford and Queen Elizabeth II.
>
> Yet Galbreath insists he's nothing special. "Just an ol' country boy. Just one of the gang."

To make the lead click, I loaded the first paragraph with as many examples of Galbreath's extraordinary success as I could pack in. That set up the "punch line" of the second paragraph: "Just an ol' country boy." Even if the reader responds with disbelief ("Yeah, right."), at least the lead elicits a response. And then the reader has to read on to see if his response was right. Reading on—that's the whole idea of the lead.

The long and short of leads

Because the lead sets up and launches into all of what's to come, it's also crucial to another old friend from part one of this book: rhythm.

The lead sets the pace; whatever comes after either follows this initial rhythm or plays off against it. Your lead starts your story fast or slow, jerky or smooth, thoughtful or theatrical.

At the most basic level, rhythm rules the ebb and flow of your lead: how it builds to a punch line, how it rolls forward into your hook and the body of your story. A staccato rhythm can act as an attention-getting gunshot at the very start of a lead, or as a contrast once the lead's got some momentum going, but one burst after another (say, a series of short sentences) can create an off-putting, beat-'em-over-the-head effect. Similarly, a series of long, languid sentences in the lead must build to some sort of release, lest the reader grow weary and wander away while your sentences wander.

The best leads combine long and short rhythms to create a pleasing effect that also, not so incidentally, mirrors the content. Here's how I started a *Travel & Leisure* story on the Black Hills of South Dakota—note the medium-length start, two longish rambles and following burst, accentuated by making it a separate, one-sentence paragraph:

> Legend has it that Paul Bunyan created the Black Hills as a burial cairn for his great blue ox, Babe. But those of a more scientific cast of mind will insist that the rough peaks of the nation's oldest mountains were made 70 million years ago, when subterranean pressure lifted a 50-mile-wide chunk of what is now South Dakota and Wyoming above the surrounding flatlands. Eons of creation have worn away the resulting dome into a crazy-quilt of granite needles, canyons studded with vivid agate, plateaus glistening with mica and rose quartz.
>
> That's what the scientists will tell you.

Not to sound like a broken record, but you can hardly miss the role of conflict and contrast in this lead. And of course the dichotomy I set up at the start—the scientific, geologic Black Hills versus the mythic place—ran throughout the article.

This is the broader role of rhythm in your lead: To underscore the themes that will play out all the way to the conclusion. The larger rhythm of my Black Hills article was a counterpoint between these disparate ways of viewing the place. So, having given the scientific viewpoint its initial due, I continued with the Indian point of view:

The Indians say the Black Hills are a sacred place, though not because any giant white man's ox is buried there. . . .

Back and forth the article went, following the rhythm inaugurated in the lead. At the end, in four bursts again accentuated by paragraphing, I brought the drumbeat of the lead to its natural conclusion:

Some say a myth is buried in these hills. The Indians say spirits dwell in the heights. They say this is a sacred place.

Perhaps they are right.

This is an ending, not a beginning, so it might seem I've strayed from this chapter's topic. But my point is that the lead can't be separated in your structure from the body of the article, or even from the end. The lead can't be a tailfin add-on. It must draw the reader into your focus, spark off the conflict and contrast of your angle, and begin the rhythm that will beat behind your story to the final word.

Paradoxically, once you understand the true importance of the lead, you'll find it easier to stop staring at that blank page and get on with your story. Every journey, as they say, begins with a single step—but it's much less daunting if you know your destination before you set out.

CHAPTER ELEVEN

Who Cares?

Getting readers beyond the bait

If your lead is like bait, a tasty nibble to get the reader's attention, what comes next must hook readers and have enough barb to keep them from slipping off. We've already seen, back in chapter two, how a "hook" or "nut graf" is an essential element of such basic structures as the "Middle Column" approach to crafting an article. But this "who cares?" ingredient is equally indispensable in articles of all sorts, from straightforward service pieces to complex and sophisticated literary journalism. You can concoct a gripping lead and do everything else right that we learned back in chapter three on "flow," but if you fail to give readers a clear and compelling hook, they will surely slip away.

Think of it in terms of simple fairness: You're asking for a substantial commitment of time and attention from a busy reader. Even a reader who's comfortably ensconced in an easy chair, receptive to your message, has a whole life full of distractions competing for his time. Other magazines, newspapers, and notes from the kid's teacher swell up around the La-Z-Boy like rough seas. The aforementioned kid is bouncing up and down on the sofa. The phone rings every seven minutes with yet another insurance pitchman. So is it too much to ask that you give the reader an unmistakable reason to read on past your lead and that you do it pretty darn soon?

The hook merely answers the reader's question: *Why should I keep reading?* This answer may be along the lines of: *What will I learn from this? Why do I need to know what you're telling me?* It could be: *What's the point here? What are you getting at?* Or maybe it's just: *What's new?* Whatever approach you take as author, however, it must include: *Why should I care?*

From focus to hook

Structurally speaking, the issues you need to grapple with concerning the hook come down to these:

1. Where does the hook come from?
2. Where does it go in the structure?
3. What form does it take?

By now you shouldn't be surprised to learn that the secret to number one is this: Your hook must spring from your story's focus and angle. If possible, this rule is even more important for your hook than for your lead; a tacked-on, tailfin hook paragraph or section is a contradiction in terms.

Indeed, your hook is all but indistinguishable from your focus and angle. Think of it as the written embodiment of the focus and angle that you settled on before you ever sat down to scribble your outline. Your hook is your decision on what your story is all about, committed to words.

For readers, this means the hook is a preview of what's to come and a promise of a payoff. Everything that follows in your article should work to support it—just as everything in your article should fit within your focus and angle.

Your hook needs to draw upon all the strengths and elements that made you select this particular focus in the first place. Keep these familiar principles from our discussion of focus in mind as they apply to your hook:

1. The hook, like your focus, should be narrow—just as a fishhook narrows to a sharp point. Don't confuse the reader with a flurry of concepts.

2. The hook should be the point at which the two ideas you are bringing into focus (Hollywood and video games, for example) actu-

ally intersect for the first time in your article.

3. Surprise is as essential to hooking the reader as it is to selecting your focus.

4. Think of your hook as a fleshing out, in full sentences, of the headline and subhead you envisioned to help establish your angle.

5. Conflict and contrast sharpen your hook, just as they do your focus.

6. If your article's focus is answering a question, the hook is the point at which you most clearly pose that question.

As we've seen, the stories in the Middle Column of *The Wall Street Journal* are textbook examples of effective "hooking"—keeping readers focused on subjects they never imagined they wanted to read about. My favorite example, which I've cited again and again in writing advice, is a *Journal* story by Barry Newman on the unlikely subject of maggots. Why keep reading about (ugh) maggots? Well, because they're bait for coarse fishing (as opposed to angling for game fish) and "coarse fishing is big in Britain, bigger than snooker. Almost four million people do it, and many others watch. Fishing matches go on television here. . . ." It's offbeat *and* it's big stuff (four million! television!). Moreover, the maggot farmer in Newman's lead turns out to be the *world champion* of coarse fishing—and the hook, of course, is where these twin ideas (maggot farming and coarse fishing) first come together in the person of the (ready?) maggot farming world champion coarse fisherman. (Whew!) So you have surprise (a famous maggot farmer!) and a superlative (world champion!), not to mention a, er, colorful character. The reader is hopelessly hooked, compelled to read on about this weird yet not insignificant combination.

Newspaper stories especially, but other timely articles as well, include the element of "what's new" in their hooks or nut grafs. If you can convince readers that your subject is really new, you're a long way toward hooking them to read on.

Other hooks work by taking the specifics of the lead and generalizing to the average reader's life. These hooks put the "you" into an article. If the story opens with a seemingly bizarre medical account, the hook must tell how this disease could strike the unwary reader at any instant. If the lead describes an amazing invention, the hook should explain how the gizmo will soon relieve drudgery right in the reader's home or office.

Hook 'em high

For the structurally savvy, the more intriguing issue regarding the hook is where to embed it in your outline. After all, since the hook springs from your focus and angle, figuring out *what* the hook ought to be is child's play—isn't it? The challenge is, rather, *where* to put this clearly stated expression of your story's purpose for maximum effect.

While you can toy with this challenge in the scribbles of your outline, the surest rule is simple: Put the hook as high up in your story as you can gracefully manage.

It is almost impossible for your hook to come too soon. If you can integrate it into your lead and both entice and hook the reader in the first few lines, by all means do so.

On the other hand, it is all too easy to bury your hook too far down in the story, so the reader loses interest before getting to your point. If editors have a universal complaint about writers and hooks (other than writers who forget the hook entirely), it's that too many writers wait too long to deliver the hook. For editors this represents a crassly practical concern: Newspaper editors want to get the hook in the opening chunk of a story (say, on the front page or on a section front), before the "jump" asks the reader to track down the rest of the copy elsewhere in the paper. If you don't get the hook before the jump, why on earth should readers be expected to hunt for the rest of a (seemingly) pointless story? Similarly, magazine editors need to get the hook before the story jumps, the reader must flip a page, or ads intervene to distract the reader's attention.

These aren't just the worries of a bunch of drones who've spent too much time sharpening their blue pencils. Good editors know their audience; it's the same audience you're striving to keep reading past your lead.

So, if in doubt, plant that hook high in the story. Look for the first logical stopping point after your lead, the first pause in the action. If your lead sets a scene or begins a narrative, you don't have to wait until the whole saga unfolds before interjecting why the reader should give a damn. Pick the point at which your opening scene veers most closely toward the heart of your focus and pounce! You can always return to the narrative flow after the hook—and your readers will thank you for answering their building question of, "Yes, this is all very interesting, but why should I care?"

The position of the hook also depends on the overall length of your nonfiction piece. If it's a multi-thousand-word opus, you can develop the lead a bit more (but only a bit!) before setting the hook; readers, conditioned by the sheer volume of pages or columns of type, won't expect a *raison d'etre* in the second paragraph. (But when you do deliver the hook for a long piece, it'd better be good!) If you've got only a thousand or so words to play with, however, you can't wait five hundred words before getting to the hook—you'll be halfway to the end. Besides risking losing the reader, placing the hook too close to the physical middle of an article distorts its function and wrecks your pacing: What follows the hook can hardly support your focus properly if what follows is little more than half of your whole.

Pure, unadulterated hook

By way of demonstrating the simple effectiveness of planting your hook high in the story, and segueing into the third (and most technically intriguing) issue at hand, namely what form the hook should take, let's look at the hook in a story I wrote for *Friendly Exchange* magazine. Think of this example as the hook in its purest, most unadulterated form. I didn't have much choice: The article had to be short—nine hundred words, tops—and yet had to tackle a densely complex topic—how Minnesota's health-care reforms might be a model for the nation. Delay more than a few paragraphs and my hook would wind up in the bottom half of the story; spread out my "who cares?" element and I'd spend more words hooking the reader than telling my tale.

Since my editor had emphasized showing the "human side" of health reform (this was in the heady days of the failed Clinton plan), I opened with a people lead: "Before MinnesotaCare, the Elliason family's health coverage consisted of hope, prayer and payment plans. . . ." After introducing the family and quoting Mrs. Elliason, I went for the hook—high in the story and packed into two straightforward paragraphs:

> But now the Elliasons and their three boys have state-subsidized health insurance, thanks to the first part of a three-pronged health-care reform that's made Minnesota a model for the nation.

MinnesotaCare, launched in October 1992, will cover 185,000 of Minnesota's 300,000 uninsured by 1997. Next, state treatment guidelines called "practice parameters" will tackle cost and quality control. And a legislative mandate for Integrated Service Networks—giant, HMO-like entities offering all medical services for a fixed, prepaid fee—begins in July 1994. The networks' plan, an example of "managed competition," aims to reduce medical inflation from 10 percent to 6 percent by decade's end.

It's no wonder Hillary Clinton visited Minnesota the week before her task force's health-care plan was unveiled. In subsequent Congressional testimony, she cited Minnesota—whose reforms are at least a year ahead of national plans—as proof the Clinton plan will work.

So what made this "who cares?" element more effective than, say, the Clinton health plan? The promised payoff for readers was straightforward: You'll learn about Minnesota's innovations and what they might mean for the nation. (Not coincidentally, this was also the assignment from the editor—my ready-made focus and angle.) Why should readers care about the Elliasons? Because what's happening to the Elliasons's health care might soon be happening to everybody.

But here the hook does more than just pique interest. It also lays out for readers a roadmap of the rest of the article. From here, I went through the three parts of the Minnesota reforms, one by one. At the end, I analyzed any lessons that the nation could draw from Minnesota's experience and, finally, returned to Mrs. Elliason's thoughts on what this means to her fellow Americans.

By mapping the rest of the article for readers, I made a complex story easier to write as well as read. I knew exactly what I had to deliver at each point in the piece—after all, I'd promised!

Three tests and three times to stretch it out

You can't go wrong, in almost any story, by following a strategy similar to my MinnesotaCare example: Place high in the story, as swiftly after your lead as possible, a clear, unambiguous statement of why the reader should care about your subject and what the payoff for reading further will be. But that doesn't mean this is the only way, or the most elegant way, to handle your hook.

An alternative to packing the "who cares?" element into one or two paragraphs is to dole it out over as many as a half-dozen or so paragraphs, weaving the hook into your narrative so the reader may never be consciously aware that he's being told why the story's worth pursuing. You might call this a "distributed hook" approach. Before you try it, however, you must make sure that your story and your arrangement of "who cares?" elements meets some basic qualifications:

1. Is the overall story long enough? In a short article, like my health-care assignment, there's just no room to spread out your hook.

2. Is your lead compelling enough to carry the readers forward into a more subtle presentation of why they should keep reading? If you have any doubts about your lead, don't take a chance on the hook.

3. Is your focus clear enough that it can be spread out without risking reader bafflement or boredom?

If in doubt on any of these points, stick with the hook in its purest, simplest form.

If you're confident about all three qualifications, you might consider a more subtle approach to hooking the reader for certain kinds of stories:

1. Stories with a strong narrative thrust. Simple storytelling power (*what happens next?*) can help drive the reader forward, while an undiluted hook stuck in the midst of a narrative can interrupt your flow. Ideally, your narrative will give you several points early on that dramatize your hook—so you can *show*, not tell, why the reader should care.

2. Stories built on a collision of two equally strong "who cares?" elements. Here you'll typically need a three-part hook strategy: one for each of the opposing forces, plus one part that brings the two together. Newman's maggot farmer/champion angler story had this kind of double whammy.

3. Stories where the reader is "pre-sold" and you can take advantage of the innate interest in your subject to dole out the hook at a more leisurely, artful pace. Stories about celebrities or those that focus on any of the basic human drives (money, sex . . .) are ripe for taking careful chances with the hook. Here your reader already cares; your task is to spell out what the payoff will be from reading this particular

article, rather than some other article, about money or sex or superstars.

For example, I once wrote a story about Rolls-Royce automobiles for *TWA Ambassador* magazine. Everybody knows the Rolls-Royce name, and it carries an aura of luxury and elegance inspiring the sort of instant envy that makes readers read on. So I didn't need a paragraph high in the story that said, "Rolls-Royce automobiles are the fanciest and most luxurious in the world . . ."

But I still needed to convince readers that my article about Rolls-Royce would deliver something they didn't already know. That became the mission of my "distributed hook."

I began with a first-person narrative of driving a Rolls through the English countryside, giving me a chance to *show* just how fancy these cars are (auto-demisting rear windows, walnut-veneer instrument panel, toothbrush-like wipers on the headlights). And I swiftly put the reader in the driver's seat by presenting a situation anybody can identify with: ". . . I am terrified of smashing up a $100,000 vehicle that I do not, alas, own."

The driving narrative also let me easily establish a sense of place that was crucial to my focus: the English countryside where Rolls-Royce automobiles are made. By the second paragraph, my promise to the reader was clear, if subtle: *I'm going to show you how a $100,000 car gets made and what in the world makes it worth $100,000.*

By the start of the third paragraph, I'd answered another important component of "who cares?"—*why now?* Yes, readers are interested in Rolls-Royce, but what's new that makes this article about Rolls-Royce worth their time now? I explained that the $100,000 model in question represented "the first all-new, four-door line to be introduced by Rolls-Royce Motors in fifteen years."

What's my hook? I never needed to state it this baldly, or in a single gulp, but it was nonetheless clear: *I'll show you how the famous Rolls-Royce auto company makes a car worth $100,000, their first such new model in fifteen years.*

And, leaving nothing to chance, I ultimately did spell out the unspoken "pre-sold" premise behind this hook: the Rolls-Royce mystique that everyone knows. After relating how the company hates references to "the Rolls-Royce of (shampoos, baby strollers, you name the product)," I wrote:

> The Rolls-Royce of automobiles is, of course, the Rolls-Royce automobile. At the pinnacle of automotive excellence, metaphor becomes tautology. This is a rare use of that comparison that Rolls-Royce, jealous of its trademark, would probably allow. . . .

Don't take the reader, or the reader's interest, for granted. That's the bottom line of the hook, whether served up in a single gulp or distributed in several portions. Every choice you make—selecting, positioning and forming the hook—must be made with the reader in mind. A skilled nonfiction writer can make the reader want to know more about any topic, whether it's Rolls-Royce autos or maggots. Answer the "who cares?" question and you've answered perhaps the greatest challenge of writing successful nonfiction.

CHAPTER TWELVE

Events and Chronology

More than merely "First this, then that"

Y ou might think it superfluous to include a chapter on "events and chronology" in a book about writing *non*fiction. Nonfiction doesn't have "events" in the same sense that fiction does—does it? Presumably, most magazine articles are compilations of facts, having more in common with a school term paper than a novel or a screenplay.

On the other hand, when things do happen in nonfiction, the writer doesn't have the fiction author's luxury of making things up or ordering events for dramatic effect. First *this* happened, then *that*. Just write it as it happened—right?

But the nonfiction writer's challenge and obligation is to craft something more interesting, more focused than real life. And that extends to events and chronology. Without changing the facts or being unfaithful to *what really happened*, the nonfiction writer—by choices in what to include and what to leave out, by ordering the unfolding of events—can and must do more than merely write "First *this* happened, then *that*."

Moreover, events can lend power and drama to even the most fact-intensive articles. Because events *show*, rather than merely *tell*, they rank high in the nonfiction writer's arsenal of ways to impart information. Wouldn't you rather have your article be a little more like a novel or a screenplay and a little less like a term paper? That's why you need to master events and chronology.

Starting points

You've probably already grappled with chronology in your lead and hook. Fundamental to your lead is the issue of where to start your story—and, as we've already seen, it doesn't necessarily have to begin at the beginning.

In fashioning your lead, you have to make two kinds of decisions about chronology:

1. When does the story start?
2. In what order should the story be told?

These questions are interrelated, but not identical, and the answers you come up with will help set the course of your chronology for the rest of your piece. Again, neither question is as obvious in its answer as you might think.

When does the story start? At the beginning, of course. Well, when is that? Let's say you're writing an article about a new treatment for heart disease that promises to reduce the need for coronary-bypass surgery. Does your story "start" with the announcement of the new treatment? With the commencement of the research that led to the treatment? Or, to better the reader's understanding of the issues at hand, should your chronology begin much further back in time—with the first bypass operation or the dawn of heart surgery or the earliest discoveries about the workings of the heart? In theory, you could begin your chain of events with the evolution of the human heart as people rose out of the primordial swamps. Isn't that, really, where your subject starts?

Yikes! This chronology business is more complicated than it seems. Fiction writers and moviemakers have to confront the same questions, of course: Does the story start with the birth of the main character (as in many nineteenth-century novels), or even with his or her parents? Or does the story not begin until our hero, say, falls in with the wrong crowd? Maybe the story encompasses just a single day, and the readers have to take the characters as they are, right now, with barely a hint of "backstory" on how they got that way. Decisions, decisions.

What you are deciding, in part, when you pick a starting point is how much of the world you're going to try to wrap your arms around. Think of the timeline of events as one of those paper chains that children make in school, except that it's a chain that extends back into time further than you can see: You must decide where to cut the chain, to slice your own chunk of story out of the whole. (You have to pick where to *end* the story, too, but that's another chapter.)

But the decisions don't end once you've got a piece of that chain in your hands. In what order should the story be told? Sure, once you've decided that the sequence of events you'll deal with begins at point A, you can simply dole out the chronology as it happened: A-B-C-D . . . and so on. But (and here's where questions of chronology become tangled with decisions about the lead) what if event A isn't the most interesting point with which to grab the reader's attention?

For instance, in our example about heart treatment, suppose that you decide the story you want to tell begins with the launch of the research project that led to this breakthrough. That's fine from a logical standpoint, but maybe not from a dramatic one. Do you really want to try to grab readers with an opening account of people unpacking lab equipment? Or, worse, a scene of filling out forms for research grants?

The best dramatic opening might be the first test of the new treatment on a human patient. That would give you a character the reader could empathize with, put a human face on abstract science, and let you *show* what's new.

In the A-B-C-D . . . chain of events, however, that terrific lead might occur at something like point E. So should you just stick with the way things happened, in order, and not risk confusing readers? Absolutely not.

Starting in the middle of things

As we saw back in chapter two, the trick of starting in the chronological middle of your story goes back to the ancient Greeks, who called it *in medias res* ("in the middle of things"). When you've got a good war to tell about, as in *The Iliad*, you don't want to have to start with the petty misunderstandings that led to the fighting; far better to launch right into the battles, then pause later in the action to bring your audience up to speed on how the fight began. (By that point, moreover, the audience will be engaged enough to *care* how it all started, chronologically.)

Applying the technique of *in medias res* to our imaginary example of an article about heart treatment, you might lead with the dramatic example of the first human patient (let's call him Joe). Next you could hook the reader by explaining how Joe Patient's successful recovery from a heart ailment could signal a surgery-free future for millions of heart patients (such as, need we add, some of the readers clogging their arteries with chips and dip while also consuming your article—talk about answering the "Who cares?" question!). By that point, readers will be intrigued and involved enough to sit through the backstory of Joe's treatment: how the research project began, where the idea for the treatment came from, the first animal trials, early setbacks and breakthroughs.

If you were to diagram the article according to our alphabetical scheme, it might go like this:

E (Joe Patient's treatment)
F (extrapolating this test to other heart patients)
A (how the research began)
B (the theories and alternatives researchers considered)
C (first animal trials)
D (early setbacks and breakthroughs leading to the first human test)

In this example, once you've caught up to the "middle of things" where you began, there's not much story left. You might go on with:

G (other human trials to date)
H (the announcement of the new treatment)
I (speculation on the future)

And that's it. "In the middle of things" can often mean starting close to the chronological end of your story; yet it can also mean picking a point only shortly after your chronological point A. Reader-grabbing appeal is the main factor in deciding where "the middle of things" lies.

It's best to pick a point *before* the dramatic climax or main revelation of your chronology. You want to start the telling before the tension is released. If we broke down our heart-treatment example even finer, for instance, you would want to start with E1 (Joe faces possible surgery) rather than, say, E4 (Joe comes through experimental surgery just fine). The difference may be no more than a couple of paragraphs, but to the reader it's all the difference in the world.

You might even want to open with Joe facing possible surgery, hook readers with the alternative of innovative treatment, *then* flash back to the beginning of the research project—leaving poor Joe in limbo until you've delivered all the necessary background. Only then would you (and the reader) return to Joe, get him through the alternative treatment, and point the way to future medical miracles for all the Joe Patients out there.

How to have a flashback

Getting from your grabber opening to the explanation of how this situation came to be (how the Trojan War was sparked, how the heart-research program began) requires a technique familiar from novels and movies—the flashback. Chronologically, a flashback is about the most radical thing you can do to your tale: You interrupt the flow of events and zip back in time to a point previous to the opening of your article, then let events start unfolding again—only now the events are, from the reader's perspective, all in the past. And at the end of the flashback you have to yank the reader forward again, past the point where the story started and all the way to where the flashback began.

You see flashbacks all the time in movies and TV shows, usually accompanied by a fogging of the screen that signals the audience, "Hey, it's a flashback, don't be confused." Writers can't fog the edges of the printed page to signal a flashback, so you have to take extra care to keep the reader oriented in time.

Because of the radical nature of the flashback and the potential for reader confusion, limit yourself to one bend in the timestream per story. As Pulitzer Prize-winner Jon Franklin puts it in *Writing for Story*, "A flashback is the most potentially disorienting technique in all the writing craft. . . . The reader usually won't stand for more than one major flashback in a story, so you've got to do it all at once." Flashbacks are not a case of one is good so two must be better. One flashback can allow you to dole out events in the most reader-grabbing order, but multiple flashbacks have the opposite effect: If the reader starts asking, "Can anybody really tell what time it is?" in the middle of your story, instead of struggling to figure it all out he'll just flip the page.

You must exercise equal caution in placing your lone flashback.

Think of our examples of *in medias res*—and of when the chronology jumps from the middle of things back to the beginning of things. It's not just as Joe Patient goes under anesthesia. As writer Jonathan Penner advises (in *Good Advice on Writing*, by William Safire and Leonard Safir), "You won't, in general, insert a flashback right in the middle of fascinating action. That merely frustrates the reader, who is trying to find out what happens next—not what happened a long time ago. But at a certain moment he will want a flashback."

When is that point, the right time to insert a flashback? Think of your article as a symphony, with movements that suggest natural pauses in-between. A flashback hits most naturally at the end of your first "movement." "Continue forward from your opening point," Penner suggests, "until the reader's curiosity about the past outweighs his curiosity about the future. . . . He'll want to know how things got like this, what makes these people the way they are. He may require orientation: time, place, relationships. This is the moment—when the story has completed its first advance—to direct the reader's attention to such anterior matters."

Getting back to the main motion of your story once the flashback is done is easier than switching to the flashback, because you are returning the reader to familiar ground. Also, as the chronology within your flashback begins to approach the chronology that's already presented (as A-B-C-D-E points toward point G, your lead), the reader will experience a satisfying glow of growing revelation: Ah, yes, this is where we came in.

The actual jump from flashback to main chronology can usually be covered with a single line or phrase of transition. An extra line of space between paragraphs can also signal the switch.

Just be clear, avoid confusing the reader, and don't flash back more than once!

Shadowing forward

The other chronological technique you may want to borrow from fiction is foreshadowing. In a sense, foreshadowing is the flip side of the flashback: Instead of inserting a chunk of the past in the middle of your story, you give the reader a taste of the future. Generally, though, foreshadowing is a much more limited, subtle playing with time than the radical lurch of a flashback. Foreshadowing is just a hint of what's to come. It may even take the form of elements that don't fully strike the reader as signs of the future until that future arrives—resulting in a pleasing "aha!" feeling of "I knew it all along."

Foreshadowing is not as common a tool in nonfiction as the flash-back, perhaps because the nonfiction writer's first rule is clarity. It's risky to make the reader guess, and there's a certain guessing-game aspect inherent in foreshadowing.

On the other hand, it can be useful to signal the reader what to expect, so he feels satisfied rather than disappointed when you arrive there together. (This is, after all, one principle of your "hook.") Sur-prise can make a story sparkle, but surprises pulled out of a hat, with no preparation, can seem like a cheat. If at the end of your article Joe Patient needs a heart transplant because sometimes the new treatment can backfire, don't wait until the second-to-last paragraph to allude to this possibility. You don't want your article to be cruising along in one direction and then veer over a cliff—at least not without warning readers that there is a cliff! That's the utility of foreshadowing for the nonfiction writer.

You can be subtle about it. Subtlety, after all, is why it's called "foreshadowing" and not "fore-blinding-the-reader-with-a-spotlight" or "fore-hammer-to-the-forehead." Suggest the existence of the cliff. Work it in sideways. As Franklin puts it, "tuck it in . . . a phrase here, a sentence there . . . the reader's subconscious mind digests before it becomes a serious issue in the story." Then, when you suddenly turn your story's steering wheel toward the cliff, the reader will know ex-actly what's happening and go along for the ride.

The reverse of this principle is Chekhov's Law, codified by the play-wright Anton Chekhov in the nineteenth century: "If the opening of a story mentions a shotgun hanging over the mantel, then that shotgun must be fired before the story ends." That is, don't mislead the reader with phony foreshadowing for cheap dramatic effect. Don't put in any details that are not essential to the point you are trying to make, to the direction your chain of events is leading.

If that sounds a lot like sticking to your focus, if it seems like all these ideas about structure and form go together—then, by George, I do believe you're getting it!

CHAPTER THIRTEEN

Exposition and Background

Smoothing the way for the facts

What's the essence of a work of nonfiction? Conveying information, of course. You might even say that *information* is the difference between nonfiction and fiction: In nonfiction, the reader expects to learn something factual. Your goal as a creative nonfiction writer may be to impart more than just the facts, but giving the reader information is an inescapable part of your job.

Ironically, though, presenting the facts can be the least interesting part of nonfiction—both for the writer and, all too often, for the reader! The facts may be essential, but that doesn't mean they're as colorful or compelling as your lead, your chronology of dramatic events, or your notebook-full of quotable quotes.

Part of the structural challenge for the nonfiction writer, then, is to craft a story that smooths the way for the facts, that lets the exposition and background go down easily. If the facts are the unavoidable medicine, the rest of an article is the spoonful of sugar—or several spoonfuls, if need be.

Pulitzer winner Richard Rhodes put the problem this way in *The Literary Journalists*: "You assume, in writing a magazine article, that the reader doesn't know. You explain, describe, list, draw analogies. By itself that would or could be boring—certainly the writing of it is boring—but that's just one layer, and it's required. Another layer is drama: plot, character, action, surprise, reversal, climax, end."

As Rhodes suggests, the key to conveying what the reader doesn't know but needs to know to make sense of it all is structure. You need to assemble the layers of your article in a way that captures the reader's attention, delivers some information, recaptures the reader, delivers some more information, and so on, all the way to the end. Properly constructed, your nonfiction should tell everything the reader needs to know without the reader even being aware that he's learning anything.

That strategy, coupled with what we've learned about flow, forms the basic dynamic of successful nonfiction. Here's how Rhodes outlines it: "The beginning of the story is almost always drama more than information, the middle is information more than drama, the end is drama again."

If this sounds familiar, it should. It follows the basic strategies we've pursued all along: Grab the reader's attention, hook him with why he should care, tell him what he needs to know, then wrap it up in a way that makes the whole more than the sum of the parts—more than just the facts.

Leaving it out

As you might guess, the first step in weaving information into your nonfiction is deciding what facts to leave out. In researching your article, you're going to discover many fascinating facts that, alas, don't have much to do with the focus of your piece. It takes enormous self-discipline *not* to put these tidbits into your story somewhere, but that's your job. If the readers simply wanted a mountain of data, they'd turn to an encyclopedia or a computer database. Instead, they're looking to you to cull the wheat from the chaff and make sense of it all.

For your own sanity, not to mention efficiency in assembling your article, the earlier you decide to leave something out, the better. Ideally, with your focus clearly in mind, you'll omit most extraneous material from your notebook altogether. While your interview subject is blathering on about some totally irrelevant issue, you should be catching up on your notetaking or thinking what to ask next to get your talk back on track—not scribbling down material you can never use. (Hence my prejudice against the tape recorder, which captures *everything* and invites you to transcribe *everything*, taking you two steps down the road to madness.) Similarly, when you hit a slow spot in a secondary source, stop taking notes or give the photocopier a rest.

The next step in winnowing your material comes as you sit down to outline. I've already suggested outlining, at first, only the points you can remember without referring to your notes; if *you* can't remember the information unprompted, chances are the reader won't find it memorable either. You should also be brutal as you scan through your notebook, looking for facts to plug into your outline. If in doubt, leave it out.

If you've stuck rigorously to your focus in notetaking and in outlining, the actual writing should be more a matter of weaving in the facts than figuring out how to cram them all in. But here, too, you should be prepared to leave some data on the cutting-room floor. At every juncture, ask yourself: Does this support what you're trying to convey (as encapsulated in your hook)? Does this fit within your focus and angle? If a fact or example is merely interesting, but not essential, resist the temptation to share it with your audience.

Packing quotes and anecdotes

All of this warning about extraneous information doesn't mean that your nonfiction should be light on facts, or that you should just make it up as you go along. Successful nonfiction comes packed with information, not filler or fluff. The writer's art lies in packaging and ordering that information to make an effortless read.

The first secret of packing your articles with information without boring the reader (after you ruthlessly eliminate every scrap of nonessential information) is combining the facts with other, more interesting elements. It's *not* just the facts, ma'am, in other words. As you outline your article, keep in mind that every piece of it must get some work done for you—quotes and colorful anecdotes, for example, can convey essential information while they entertain and inject drama. (If you're doing it right, you'll see it in your outline: At the point where you plan to place a quote or anecdote, you'll have other essential information noted that you want to impart in the process. Instead of one item per paragraph, you might have two or three.) Nobody wants to read big globs of facts unenlivened by personality or perspective. So tuck in those tidbits when you've got your reader's attention!

Quotes are a way of telling the reader something in an interesting chunk of words. By putting the facts in another person's voice, you add color and personality to the bare bones of the data. Here's an example from the story I did about Rolls-Royce automobiles:

"The work varies. It can be anything any day; a radiator shell for any Rolls, one back for repair that's been damaged in an accident. That doesn't happen too often," Dennis adds. "It's a box, isn't it? And, being a box, it's very strong."

Sure, I could have conveyed the same information in a much more straightforward fashion, using fewer words:

The work of a grillmaker varies from day to day, ranging from crafting a new radiator shell to repairing one damaged in an accident. But the boxlike Rolls-Royce is strong, so accident damage is rare.

That's all right, but it's missing a chance to engage the reader while imparting information. Moreover, the tone of the quotation tells the reader something beyond bare facts, something about the matter-of-fact pride the company takes in its products.

On the other hand, don't make the speakers in your quotations do all your dirty work for you. Globs of statistics, even if you heard them from an interviewee's mouth, don't make for colorful quotes. You must strike a balance between economy of words and the liveliness of the telling; too much of either makes for unreadable articles.

Like quotes, anecdotes and narrative make information go down easily. You can pack plenty of facts into action—remember the rule to show, not tell. Here's how I opened that Rolls-Royce story, as I've already alluded in chapter eleven:

The roads in and around Crewe, in west-central England, are a labyrinth of hedges, narrow stone bridges, parked cars fully blocking one lane of a barely two-lane motorway. We are just 40 miles southwest of Manchester, 50 miles southeast of Liverpool, three hours north on the M1 and M6 superhighways from London. These roads have been intimate with cattle for more years than with modern traffic. I am weaving a brand-new, claret-red Rolls-Royce Silver Spirit through the hedgerows. I am trying to remember to stay on the left-hand side of the road without staying so far left that the sideview mirror (electronically adjustable from the car's interior) trims unruly bushes as we pass. Not that this car is difficult to handle. It is the nearest thing, in smoothness, to hang-gliding on the ground. It responds to my steering as I imagine Trigger must have heeded Roy Rogers's slightest commands. No, the reason I am feeling anything other than *The Spirit of Ecstasy* promised in the name of the hood ornament sweeping the scenery before me is precisely that this car is so free from fault, and I am terrified of smashing up a $100,000 vehicle that I do not, alas, own.

Let's take a quick inventory of the information I was able to get across while entertaining the reader with my driving escapade (*will this idiot crack up this expensive dream car?*):

• The location of Crewe (where, as the next paragraph will make clear, Rolls-Royce cars are made)
• The rural setting
• A sense of the car's amenities
• The car's superb steering
• The name of the famous hood ornament
• The price tag

All this while getting my article rolling! Unleavened facts can make a story grind to a halt, but your exposition and background—if properly woven into quotes or anecdotes—can also make your writing move. Remember that the reader wants to know *why* (if your lead and hook do their jobs), so you do have a receptive audience. Just don't try to unload all the *why* at once.

Balancing "sizzle" and exposition

Generally the most challenging chunk of exposition and background is the one that comes shortly after your hook. The good news at this crucial point is that you've piqued the reader's interest to the maximum. The bad news is that, after a lot of reader-attracting sizzle, suddenly you have to start serving up some steak. The transition between enticing the reader and delivering the goods can be tricky, and many articles lose their flow in the process.

The temptation is to segue from lead and hook into a long expository section. The reader needs to know this stuff to understand the point you're making, so here goes!

On the other hand, you can't tilt to the opposite extreme and eschew essential background information altogether, or postpone it to the tail end of your tale. The reader really does need some filling in about now, to ward off confusion and to make sense of what's ahead.

So you must strike a delicate balance. And you must, wherever possible, weave in even this post-hook stretch of facts through quotes, anecdotes and action.

We saw back in chapter eleven how I made the hook of my Rolls-Royce story explicit ("The Rolls-Royce of automobiles is, of course, the Rolls-Royce.") and then began to substantiate it. It's that substantiation that gets dicey, because here the reader is going to demand proof—facts, in other words. I could get away with relatively unadulterated facts for four paragraphs here, because the facts themselves were pretty sexy: celebrities who had owned Rolls-Royces, Lawrence of Arabia's praise for the car, the colors of Queen Elizabeth's five Rolls-Royce Phantoms (all Royal Claret—and permission from Her Majesty must be obtained by anyone else desiring that shade).

But even on a subject so spectacular, I swiftly opted to mix some quotes and narrative in with the raw data. After the celebrity paragraphs, I injected some personality:

> Other facts on Rolls-Royce ownership are not readily forthcoming. "We just don't talk about that sort of thing. It's their business, really."

I stuck with quotation for the next, longish paragraph, about bulletproofing the cars. Then I made a transition into the backstory of the origins of the company, telling it as a mini-saga of "a poor miller's son from Awalton," Henry Royce. Facts (how many models and how many automobiles the company has made since 1904) fell into place within the unfolding story of Royce and his upper-crust partner, Charles Rolls.

By the end of this segment, I'd brought the backstory up to almost the present day and presented some essential history plus business and engineering statistics. The overall section was structured like this:

- *4 paragraphs:* The most colorful chunks of information that support the hook
- *2 paragraphs:* Quotes on the company, celebrities and special cars
- *8 paragraphs:* From rags to riches

And then I was ready to jump back to my present-day scene, the factory in Crewe where these cars (including the one I'd just been navigating through the hedgerows) are created. It's not just that I needed to deliver those fourteen paragraphs of background for the reader to get the whole story—I needed the background there to support my hook, to make the reader care about where Rolls-Royces come from.

But I didn't need, at that point, for the reader to know *everything* about the company. I held some background in reserve, balancing the reader's need to understand and give a damn with the danger of losing flow and reader interest. Explaining the company's near-fatal financial troubles in the 1970s, for instance, could wait until after a preliminary tour through the factory. Some local color, lively quotes from proud craftsmen, more examples of the extremes to which this auto maker goes to make the best car in the world . . . *then* the reader would sit still for more backstory: "It was not 'the best car in the world' that broke Rolls-Royce Ltd. In 1971 . . ."

The nonfiction writer's task in delivering facts and background is not unlike that of a composer of music. Not too much *pianissimo*—but not too much *fortissimo*, either, lest the audience flee with their hands over their ears. The composer uses notes; the nonfiction writer uses facts. Both can create something beautiful—and memorable.

CHAPTER FOURTEEN

Quotes

Using good quotes

Quotations can be among the most powerful weapons in the nonfiction writer's arsenal. Simply reporting the words of your subjects as they said them can add immediacy, drama and credibility to your articles.

As John Brady observes in his superb *The Craft of Interviewing* (a must for any nonfiction writer's bookshelf), "Today's reader wants more than bare facts—he wants to know why an event occurred, what feelings it incited, how it might have been avoided. Editors demand journalists who know more than just the card tricks of writing, who know how to probe their interviewees for that telling detail, the taut quote. Many editors consider the best interviewers to be, inescapably, the best writers."

But before you race out with notebook and tape recorder in hand, please note this as well: "Getting good quotes," as editors like to put it, approvingly, is only half the battle. Using quotes effectively once you've got them can be just as tricky as squeezing a killer quote out of a reluctant interviewee.

"Simply" reporting the words of your subjects, in short, isn't as simple as it seems: Using quotes right is one of the nonfiction writer's greatest challenges in assembling a story. Quotes can give life to an article—or suck the life right out of it. It's all in how you use quotes, how much you use them, and how you order them (remember rhythm?). The most dynamite, heart-tugging, gasp-inducing quotes won't explode on the page, tug heartstrings or get gasps if they're buried, broken up or deflated. Too heavy a reliance on direct quotation can make your article read like a monologue. Awkward use of these snippets of real talk can confuse the reader *(who's talking now?)*, submerge your focus in a flood of irrelevant verbiage, and risk redundancy.

Getting "good quotes," in short, isn't enough. Even the most successful, probing, tactically brilliant interviewer must also learn how to effectively weave those good quotes into the structure of a story.

The power of the real stuff

The power of direct quotation springs from its immediate link with reality. Putting those " " marks around words signals the reader: *You are there. This is exactly what you would have heard if you'd been in my shoes. This is the real stuff.*

But this means you must live up to your end of the bargain implied by those " " marks. You must quote your subjects accurately and fairly, capturing not only what they said but how they said it.

Properly used, this dose of reality can give your articles immediacy, immersing readers in the action. Direct quotations add authority and authenticity—readers will trust what you write when it's in the subject's own voice. And quotes inject personality, when your subject says something more colorfully, colloquially or vividly than you the author could get away with. You might write, "He was depressed." But your subject might say, "My dobber was really down." Even using the same words, direct quotations pack more punch than authorial pronouncements. Compare:

> It was the greatest day of her life.
> "It was the greatest day of my life," she says.

But there's a downside, too, to the fidelity of direct quotation, a downside that gets to the heart of the trickiness of integrating quotes into your story structures. Most of the time, most of what people say doesn't fall under the heading of "good quotes." Even the best interview subject can be rambling and inarticulate, repetitive and downright boring in the long stretches between "good quotes." Just as you must select the key facts to include in your story, so too must you pick and choose among the torrent of words resulting from even a brief phone interview.

Many writers, even experienced ones, tape their interviews and then sit and transcribe the entire encounter. Of the dozens of pages of quotations laboriously transcribed, only a page or two—scattered throughout the transcript—should actually wind up in a finished article. Nobody is quotable for sentence after sentence, page after page! Yet the act of committing these quotes to paper (or computer file) makes it much harder to be selective. After you've gone to all the work of typing a quote, it seems wasteful for it not to wind up in your finished story.

That's how interview-intensive stories get to be unreadable, unfocused piles of quotations. Unless you do your job as sifter, filterer and shaper, the story reads just like real life—and just as boring. Hence the common criticism from editors, "It's just a bunch of quotes strung together."

Taking the right notes: "Get this down!"

Though quotes can pack more punch than many other article elements, and though they carry a special cachet (and burden) of authenticity, you must orchestrate your quotes as part of an overall structural strategy. So you should think about quotes the same way that we looked at all the elements of your article back in chapter nine, on outlining. From the very beginning of your research, including your first interview, you should work toward the vital moment when it all comes together in your outline.

That means getting the most out of your good quotes starts with identifying them in your notebook and with weeding out the useless quotes. When taking notes in an interview, I always keep in mind my article's focus and my objectives for the interview; if something the subject says doesn't fit my focus, I don't write it down. I also try to differentiate, on the fly, between facts and figures gleaned from an interview and colorful quotes. If an interviewee is rattling off census statistics or dates, the most important thing is to get those facts right in your notes; the exact words in-between the facts are less crucial, since such material is unlikely to make for juicy direct quotes. These strategies not only help my scribblings keep up with the conversation, but they make for less excess verbiage to weed through when outlining.

On the other hand, when a good quote starts to come out of my subject's mouth, an internal alarm goes off. "Get this down!" it screams at me. "This is good stuff!" (Keeping my focus firmly in mind helps me recognize a choice quote when I hear one.) Really good quotes get a quick slash down the side in my notebook, to highlight them for ready retrieval.

Later, I'll review my notes and mark more quotes I'm likely to use—but only after I've sketched out my overall structure. Knowing where my article is going and more or less how it will get there helps me spot quotes that will do some of the work I've laid out. It also keeps me from being tempted by well-turned phrases that nevertheless don't relate to the point of my article.

Each candidate for direct quotation gets noted, by notebook page number, in my outline, just as I flag standout statistics or anecdotes. Once I've got a good quote and a spot to use it, I don't want to have to hunt for it in the creative throes of composition.

Building your story like a fence—interlocking pieces that must stretch from here to there—rather than chopping it out of a forest of unfocused notes also forces you to think about what work each quote does for you. For quotes, just like facts, must do some of the work of storytelling. They might be fence posts or rails or merely nails, but they can't be mere decoration.

Putting quotes to work

What kind of work can good quotes do for your story? As I've already hinted, quotes can convey information mixed with emotion. (They're not particularly efficient, on the other hand, for imparting big doses of pure facts.) The selection of words in a quote can characterize the speaker, often more subtly yet effectively than any description by you; choice quotes let you "show, not tell." Quotes can humanize a set of facts, linking the general situation you've described to a specific person—part of another crucial challenge facing the nonfiction writing, moving from the general to the particular.

If you remember that quotes can do some of your story's work, you'll be less likely to fall into the trap of quote redundancy. Too often writers first summarize a quote, then give the actual quote:

The new program aims to make claims processing more efficient. "Our goal is to get claims processed with less time and manpower," Smith says.

Let the quote say it, or you say it—but not both. If in doubt, skip the direct quotation and save this weapon for places where you really need it. You can often say it more succinctly than your source. And too much blah-blah-blah quotation robs your good quotes of their impact. If everything is between quotation marks, you lose that special signal to the reader; your subjects' voices take over from yours.

What else can quotes do better than ordinary exposition? Direct quotes also work for humor, irony, drama, understatement and revelation. Let the subject tell the joke; it will be funnier. And it will be more effective to let a subject skewer himself with his own words than for you to play judge. Quotes can express the drama of a situation more powerfully than paraphrase can. Properly set up, quotes can say more through understatement than you can convey with your most overwrought phrasings:

Standing in the hole that once was her living room, Jones says, "Yep, it was a mighty big blast."

And when your subject has a confession to make, a moment of self-realization, readers want to hear it in the subject's own words:

"When I realized I'd put my own child in the hospital," Anderson says, "I decided it was time I get some help."

Handling attribution: Who said that?

All of these uses also affect the rhythm of your writing. Quotes break up your page, both visually and in the reader's "ear." (Too many unbroken quotes, in turn, make for a page that needs an interruption by the author's voice.) A short, humorous quote can counterbalance a weighty paragraph of exposition. Quotes can work as punch lines, delivering on your narrative setup. Or quotes can be a counterpunch, a contrast to what's gone before.

Switching to direct quotation is like changing the window the reader is looking through. You're shifting from a view of the facts to a viewpoint on the facts. (This is technically true of indirect quotation as well, but the impact on the reader of those quotation marks is more than just a matter of degree.) Quotes can invite the reader to argue with the speaker, or reach for the reader's sympathies.

This impact on rhythm and on, if you will, the "pitch" of a story is why attribution becomes such a tricky issue with direct quotes. As your lone intrusion into the raw stuff of a quotation, attribution—the "he said, she said"—must go with the flow of a quote, not block or interrupt it. In general, your goal should be to make attribution as invisible and seamless as possible; make clear who's talking, as early yet unobtrusively as you can, and then get out of the way. If you've done your homework and selected only the choicest quotes, let them speak for themselves.

Usually the best place to sneak in an attribution is after the first point in a quote where the reader and the speaker "take a breath." This may be at the end of the initial sentence, if it's brief, or after the first phrase or clause:

> "We've come a long way," says Peterson. "Our experiments with cold fusion. . . ."

or

> "The most important thing to remember," Weiss says, "is that we're dealing with human lives here."

Sometimes you can start a quote with the attribution. This works if there's no natural pause early in the quote, or if the quote builds slowly to a climax and the attribution serves as a low-key launching pad.

The first time that a subject speaks, or when you are quoting several subjects in the same section of an article, it's important to work in the attribution as early and as clearly as possible. Never leave the reader guessing who's speaking. And, if in doubt, err on the side of over-attribution rather than risking confusion.

Except for very brief quotes, where there's no natural internal pause, ending with the attribution fritters away most of the benefits of rhythm and pitch gained with a direct quote. The attribution becomes a little tail at the end of the quote, with nothing to make it wag. The effect is flattening, anticlimactic:

". . . All of which makes this one of the most crucial events in human history," the professor said.

Remember that sentences tend to build toward an emphasis at the end; sticking the attribution there gives a false emphasis on the matter-of-fact "he said."

In particular, ending your entire article with an attribution robs a carefully chosen closing quote of its dramatic force.

You'll note that all my imaginary examples employ "says" or "said." Of course you already know that such a simple attribution is almost always preferable to "laughed" or "expostulated" or "retorted" or "ejaculated." Don't you? Obviously, if you're striving to keep out of the way of good quotes, the last thing you'd want is a distracting verb.

As you can see by now, it's a delicate business, this delivering raw doses of real life. John Brady, with whom we began this chapter, closes the main portion of *The Craft of Interviewing* with a reminder that while the writing comes second to the interviewing chronologically, the writer must write as carefully as he frames questions—"lest the truth and color of his material leak away before reaching print."

And Brady concludes, "For when he writes with clarity and fire—with a piece of himself—he will not merely inform the reader, as any piece of research would. He will move him."

(What better way to end this chapter, after all, than with a quote?)

CHAPTER FIFTEEN

Sentences and Paragraphs

The building blocks of structure and flow

Once you've got a handle on your lead and your hook, charted the sequence of events and the facts you need to impart, and chosen your choicest quotes, eventually you must get down to the hard work of actually putting these elements on paper. Sentences and paragraphs are the basic building blocks of structure and flow. Here is where everything you know about flow and contrast, unity and rhythm gets put to work. And here is where all too many writers veer off course, letting the best-laid plans of their outlines turn into unwieldy and unreadable prose.

So before we look at how to link the chunks of your writing together (transitions) or how to end your nonfiction, let's pause and reflect on the atoms and molecules of your articles: the humble sentence and the lowly paragraph.

I don't mean writing a grammatical sentence or a paragraph in which all the words are spelled right. And I'm not talking about mastery of punctuation, knowing where to put a period to end a sentence. Those skills are part of the price of admission.

No, understanding structure and flow at this fundamental level means crafting sentences that work hard, paragraphs that get maximum mileage for the expenditure of words. Ultimately, an article is just one sentence after another and then one paragraph after another.

So how do you structure sentences that sing and paragraphs that, while they may not necessarily live up to every expectation of your grammar-school English teacher, nonetheless corral your ideas in ways that work for readers?

Ten ways to make sentences work

Let's start with the sentence, building from smaller parts to larger. While I hate to lay down rules—remembering that they're made to be broken—I can offer some, er, strong suggestions on structuring your sentences. We're trying to make your sentences robust, hard-working, so the focus here will be on keeping the flab out of these basic building blocks of prose.

Can you ever break these strong suggestions? Of course, and every good writer does. But do it consciously, for a reason. Know that you're taking a stylistic chance with a sentence, to achieve a particular effect or build a certain rhythm. Don't commit sentence-structure sins out of ignorance or sloth. Know what you're doing first; then you can turn up the Bunsen burner and see what other tricks the writing lab might hold.

With that caveat, here are ten strong suggestions for structuring better sentences:

1. *Don't begin with "There is" or "There are."* I'll confess, this is a pet peeve of mine. There are few weaker ways to start a sentence than "There is" or "There are."

See what I mean? The lifeless "there," a word devoid of information or action, starts your sentence going nowhere. Following with a form of "to be," rather than an action verb, keeps your sentence in neutral. By this point you're at word three and have yet to tell the reader a thing!

Instead of "There are few weaker ways to start a sentence than 'There is' or 'There are,' " try: "Starting a sentence with 'There is' or 'There are' sucks the life out of whatever follows." Or: "Avoid starting your sentences in neutral with the directionless 'There is' or 'There are.' "

2. *Opt for active voice.* A spiritual kin of "There is," passive voice likewise drains the zip from your sentences. Passive voice is the language of bureaucrats, ivory-tower academics and Pentagon paper-

pushers. Passive voice reverses the English language's good old "subject-verb-object" scheme and makes events happen before their causes.

That model of powerful English prose, the King James Bible, shows a clear understanding that "Thou shalt not use passive voice" would have been commandment number 11 if Moses hadn't had to hurry down the mountain. Consider the opening line: "In the beginning, God created the heavens and the earth." A bureaucrat or other writer infected with passive voice would have written, "In the beginning, the heavens and the earth were created by God."

3. *Pick punchy verbs.* "Verbs," notes William Zinsser, "are the most important of all a writer's tools." So why do so many writers weigh down their sentences with wimpy, punchless verbs?

Consider another example from the King James Bible: "Moses lifted up his hand, and with his rod he smote the rock twice." "Smote" isn't a verb we use much nowadays, but it's a darned good one and maybe worth resurrecting. "Lift," "smite," "jump," "grin"—our language sparkles with potent verbs that put a picture in the reader's head. But see how that biblical sentence reads with its verbs anesthetized: "Moses made an upward motion of his hand, and used his rod to impact the rock twice."

4. *Eschew needless words.* Don't use three or four words when one will do; don't use empty words ("quite a few," "rather") when none will do. Don't write "the reason why is that" when the simple "because" will suffice. Don't waste your time even typing "the fact that." Ruthlessly rub out "little" and "pretty" unless you're referring to size and beauty.

Strunk and White, in their indispensable *The Elements of Style*, call such clutter "the leeches that infest the pond of prose, sucking the blood of words."

5. *Use adverbs cautiously.* Rely on your ears and your eyes, not the random insertion of words ending in "-ly." Let quotations stand on their own, for example, without phrases such as "he said glumly" or "she opined hopefully." Stick to an unadorned "he said" and "she said," or attach an action to the quote: "he said, wadding the report into a ball and flicking it across the room."

6. *Spare the adjectives.* Like adverbs, adjectives must hitch a ride on your nouns and verbs; overload a sentence with adjectives and the

whole contraption goes nowhere. Keep in mind these words of Mark Twain: "Thunder is good, thunder is impressive, but it is lightning that does the work." You can thunder all you like with adjectives, but it's nouns and verbs that do the zapping.

That doesn't mean you should skip descriptions when forming your sentences. But let the facts, not your thesaurus, do the work. Instead of writing that a man is "tall," say that he's "six-foot-four." Instead of describing a profile subject's desk as "cluttered," list some of the things that clutter it, each of which in turn adds information: computer disks, dog-eared copies of *The Wall Street Journal,* a bottle of Maalox—get the picture?

7. *Stick with specifics.* It's not just in your use (or avoidance) of adjectives that you should veer toward the specific and the concrete. Details, numbers (not "a lot" but "137"), quotes, names, sensory specifics all make sentences sparkle.

Listen (yes, *listen,* because effective sentences make a music in the mind) to Sydney Lea, founder of the *Bread Loaf Quarterly,* describe the beginning of a grouse-hunting trip in a piece for *The Virginia Quarterly Review*: "Behind the creamery, land plummets down a steep lane of haw and blasted apple. I follow. A blaze flares from a trunk where a buck has hooked, and here and there his cuff marks and the orange dribble of his rut show as I wobble downhill." If you'll pardon the adjective indulgence, that's vivid, vigorous writing; the sentences catch in your brain as clearly as the mark of the buck. What if instead Lea had written: "Behind the building, the land goes downhill among some trees. I go down there. I see some signs of a buck on and around a tree as I walk downhill"? Bleah!

8. *Don't be afraid to use the period.* William Faulkner could get away with sentences that ramble on for pages, but he was Faulkner. Express one thought, then end your sentence. Spend another sentence on the next thought, and so on.

Too many short sentences is as bad as too many long sentences, but somehow that's a less-common failing. Remember our chapter on rhythm? You've gotta have it.

9. *Watch out for backward sentences.* Wolcott Gibbs nailed this sin against strong sentences in a critique of the stilted "Time-ese" of Henry Luce's *Time, Life* and *Fortune* magazines of the 1950s: "Backward ran sentences until reeled the mind." (He concluded his skewering with:

"Where it will all end, knows God!")

Check your sentences for this symptom of stilted structure. Your sentences should read as though you were saying them to a friend, not as though you were making a speech to an academic gathering.

10. *End on a strong note.* Strunk and White advise placing your most prominent or important words at the end of your sentence, for emphasis. Because this ultimate word or phrase is typically the new idea introduced by the sentence, this strategy also pushes your prose along—from one new idea to the next.

To take one last example from the Bible, think of how the commandments are structured: "Thou shalt not kill." *Killing* is the point of this sentence, as in *don't do it,* so the word "kill" waits till the end. Much weaker would be: "Killing is something thou shalt not do"—by the time the sentence finishes, you've forgotten what you're not supposed to do!

The basic unit of composition

Strunk and White, who seem to be star players in this chapter, also had something to say about the next step up from sentences—the paragraph. In *The Elements of Style*, they advise relying on the paragraph as the basic unit of composition.

Your elementary-school teachers probably said much the same thing, only more so. Paragraphs, we all learned in grade school, must be built from topic sentences, with each sentence thereafter serving to support the topic.

If you've done much writing, or looked closely at almost any published article, you know that it ain't necessarily so. Study the choppy paragraphing of most newspaper writing, for instance, and you'll conclude that topic sentences must have gone out with hot type.

The art of the paragraph in nonfiction is a flexible thing, far from the strict lessons of grammar school. But that doesn't mean you should throw the baby out with the bathwater. However liberated from rules and conventions, no matter how changeable, depending on the medium, the paragraph remains a useful structural tool both for writers and their readers.

For the writer, though you need not be strictly bound by topic sentences, the paragraph can indeed be a useful unit of composition.

Thinking about your work in the convenient "chunks" of paragraphs makes for more manageable organizing. The paragraph is simply practical: Most articles require too many individual sentences to keep them all straight in your head as you're trying to decide which comes where; as the next bigger unit, the paragraph makes an ideal building block for assembling articles. As we've seen, paragraphs spring naturally from the organizing approach of an outline, neatly holding one or several points from your plan.

For the reader, the paragraph offers a welcome spot to catch a breath. It breaks up the grayness of a page and makes a long column of type seem less intimidating.

Herein lies the source of the sometimes-dramatic difference in paragraphing between newspapers and magazines or books. A newspaper, built for rapid scanning, must present a bite-sized look to the wary reader; magazines, particularly those aimed at a more settled-in-the-easy-chair audience, such as the *Atlantic* and *The New Yorker*, can get away with bigger blocks of type. Newspapers, too, generally have narrower columns, making *Atlantic*-esque paragraphs stretch down the page like gray skyscrapers. The result is what William Safire calls "hyperparagraphication" in newspaper prose: "like feeding a baby tiny spoonfuls of mashed banana, building an appetite between insertions of the spoon in the ready-to-squawl mouth."

How can you strike a balance between building your story out of well-constructed paragraphs and keeping the reader from squawling? In the absence of the old rules, it helps to keep in mind several up-to-date organizing principles for successful paragraphing. The labels are mine; if your grandchildren read them one hundred years from now, set down in a schoolbook as strict rules, please forgive me. . . .

New rules for paragraphing

First and most sweeping is what we might dub the **modified grammar-school approach**. That is, while your paragraphs need not be constructed in a strict topic-support-support hierarchy, it is still useful to think of each paragraph as making a point—just *one* point.

If you're writing a travel article about Seattle, for instance, you might have a spot in your outline where you want to mention Seattle's proximity to the Washington State wine industry. The paragraph growing out of this point could be built like this:

Seattle as a place to sample Washington State wine industry
1. Chateau Ste. Michelle winery
2. Columbia Crest winery

Each specific winery might consume a sentence or two, with a few facts about its setting, tastings and tours. The whole paragraph, with setup sentence and specifics, would take four or five sentences—a manageable glob on most pages, readily consumed by even fickle readers.

By forming your paragraphs this way, each becomes a quasi-independent unit of thought, easily manipulated as you write and rewrite. In our make-believe story on Seattle, your paragraph on wineries might be woven into a discussion on things to see and do in the city's outer reaches. Suppose you decided instead that Seattle's winery connections would fit more smoothly into a larger section on the city as a mecca for gourmets? Pick up the paragraph and move it! Or maybe you conclude that your article's main focus ought to be on Seattle as a fun place for families, and wineries don't really fit after all. Select that paragraph and use the delete key.

Paragraphs that follow the modified grammar-school approach work like a child's Lego building blocks. Even before they are completely written, you can easily try them out in other locations, test their fit with other paragraphs, and move them to make new connections. They are also handy units for combining into larger, more complex structures—without having to worry whether each component part will hold up under the stress of composing the whole.

The modified grammar-school approach will also keep you clear of the extremes of hyperparagraphication—those stories made up of single-sentence paragraphs streaming across the page like machine-gun fire. (In such a story, the sentence about Seattle and wineries plus the citation of each individual winery would each be a separate paragraph. That's a good way to wear out your return key, not to mention the reader.)

But once you start gathering elements together to form paragraphs, it's easy to tilt to the opposite extreme: Like a snowball rolling downhill, your paragraphs keep accreting until the reader gets buried in an avalanche of unbroken sentences. The cure for such megaparagraphs comes from recognizing the natural pauses and logical breaks in your prose. These aren't mandatory paragraphing spots, but your readers will thank you if, when in doubt, you hit the return key.

Start with an extension of the grammar-school strategy—think of it as the **enumeration break**. Whenever you have a subsidiary point to make that will take more than a sentence or two to explain or illustrate, make it a new paragraph. Whenever you have a list (four things to remember about proper paragraphing, six must-see attractions in downtown Seattle), consider whether each element in the list will occupy more than one sentence. If so, make each element its own paragraph.

You can envision the enumeration break as resulting in paragraphs like this:

The first thing . . .
Second, . . .
A third factor . . .

And so on—though it's not necessary to actually number your points.

A related invitation to hit the return key is the **elaboration detour**. Think of it as akin to the enumeration break but with only one subpoint. Essentially, you are detouring from the main march of your argument to elaborate for the length of a paragraph on one aspect of the previous paragraph. Take, for example, the relationship between the two paragraphs above: one introducing the concept of the enumeration break, the other presenting a helpful way to think about it.

You might use this elaboration detour to separate a general paragraph (Seattle has many attractions for the gourmet) from a specific illustration of an element of that paragraph (for example, wineries). By setting off the example in its own paragraph, you give the reader a break and signal your small directional shift.

Detours that take the reader in an opposite direction, of course, demand a new paragraph. This is the **on-the-other-hand switcheroo**. Here the brief breather of a new paragraph prepares the reader for an idea in contrast to what has gone before.

The on-the-other-hand switcheroo works with opposing viewpoints, balancing opinions and cautionary notes. Need to inject a bit of not-so-fast-folks? Interweaving differing perspectives on an issue? Presenting the pros and cons? A paragraph switcheroo warns the reader of your bend in the road.

To use the on-the-other-hand switcheroo, look for signs of contrasting thoughts such as:

But . . .
. . . however . . .
And yet . . .
(As well as, of course:) On the other hand . . .

But the breaks in your story don't have to be as dramatic as divergent opinions. (Note the switcheroo there that practically begged for a new paragraph?) You should keep your authorial ear tuned for any sort of interruption in the action that can serve as a basic **paragraphable pause.**

Quotations are the most obvious example of a shift that calls for a new paragraph. With each new speaker, or alternation in speaker, hit the return key. Just as your speakers catch their breath between speeches, so too should you let your readers rest with the tiny space of a fresh paragraph.

Other opportunities for paragraphable pauses abound. Switches of your authorial camera between persons, even if they're not speaking, let you switch paragraphs as well. In an article with a chronological aspect, you might seize on a shift in time to start a new paragraph: the next day, an hour later, at 8 P.M., and so on. Even minor changes of place call for a change of paragraph: farther down the street, across the highway, on the other side of the room.

You can take advantage of the small pause, the break in rhythm, created by a fresh paragraph to emphasize what follows—even when the reader might not be expecting a break. This **emphatic paragraphing** works like the print equivalent of a dramatic pause in speaking: Whatever comes after gains weight and import from the artificial break. It is set apart, put in the spotlight.

Typically, emphatic paragraphing is used to set off paragraphs of only a sentence or two. The power of a suddenly new paragraph quickly dissipates over the span of several sentences. A short burst of a paragraph, on the other hand, gains potency not only from its indentation but from the visual variety on the page.

The emphatic paragraph can be a single dramatic statement, a quote, even a question such as:

Was everything I thought I knew about paragraphs wrong?

The answer to that question, as you can see, is: Not exactly. The basic principles of one-topic-per-paragraph and unit-of-composition still apply; contemporary nonfiction writing has just bent the rules to keep the interest of impatient readers and to add bounce and variety to prose. The paragraph, like the sentence, remains a writer's basic tool of structure and flow.

Now you just need to figure out how to link those paragraphs together, which requires making a transition to our chapter on transitions . . .

CHAPTER SIXTEEN

Transitions

Getting readers from here to there

After errors of spelling and punctuation, perhaps the most common problem for an editor to cite on a manuscript is a weak, illogical or missing transition. In the days of blue pencils, before electronic editing, I used to scribble "tr." in the margin of many a manuscript. Sometimes it was "tr?" or even "tr!" and accompanied by vigorous arrows indicating my displeasure at the writer's failure to make clear the path from here to there.

The reason editors harp on transitions is because these logical links are so vital to getting the reader from here to there. Remember that transition gaps are one of the chief culprits in interrupting flow and giving the reader an invitation to escape.

And yet writers don't always seem to care about transitions. *You* know how it all fits together, and why this section comes after that one, so it's all too easy to skip some of the stitching that holds one piece to another. Writers can become like impatient tailors, so eager to complete the suit and so sure of their vision that they forget to mind their sewing. When the reader tries it on for size, the sleeves fall off.

But transition gaps can also short-circuit the writer's creative flow. If you're ever afflicted with writer's block, a transitional trip-up is a sure way to bring on a full-blown case. You know what you have to write next, but you can't figure out how to start writing it because there's no clear way to get from what you've already written to what you need to write next.

Fortunately, advance attention to structure and flow can solve many of your transition woes before they reach the page. If you've structured your story along a clear focus and outlined your component parts to support that focus, the pieces you must write will naturally fall into place. Labored, awkward transitions, however, are a sure sign of a badly structured article. It's like the difference between a road builder who starts pouring asphalt only after careful surveying and a builder who just starts laying down road, hoping he'll wind up someplace drivers want to go. If you don't have a map, chances are that you'll have to bridge some chasms along the way.

No amount of transitional trickery can paper over genuine gaps in your structure. If you find yourself writing long, strained links between sections of your story, the only cure is to go back to your outline and reorganize until the sections not only seem to connect with each other, but do.

That said, as you fine-tune and tweak your structure, you *can* make strategic choices that ease the writing of transitions. Your goal, after all, is not just smoothness but seamlessness. As Jon Franklin puts it in *Writing for Story*, "the best transition . . . is the one that doesn't exist—as when a clever writer ends [a section] with an image that will send the reader's mind leaping automatically toward the first image in the next."

So how do you go about crafting transitions that seem not to exist—but *do*, pulling the reader irresistibly along? Let's look at three transition techniques that can help you keep the sleeves on your story.

The logic of lists

The most basic transition technique, and the one most fundamentally tied to your article's structure, is a variation on the list: If you first create an expectation in the reader's mind, then he will feel satisfaction, not confusion, when that expectation is satisfied. Look at the last sentence of the previous paragraph, for example; I've primed the reader to expect three techniques—a glorified list. Now I don't have to worry about making the transition from technique number one to technique number two; it's already set up in the reader's mind.

This list-like approach is ideally suited to nonfiction. If you have a number of points to cover, several gobs of information to impart, the simplest structure is one point right after another. Say you're writing an article about "Five Old West Cities for New West Fun." The structure that immediately suggests itself is:

1. Dallas
2. Denver
3. Reno
4. San Antonio
5. Santa Fe

You simply write about each city in turn; the reader, expecting a list of five, never wonders what the heck you are doing when you jump from one city to the next. If you chose instead, say, to intermingle the five cities' attributes—writing a section about restaurants in all five, a section about tourist attractions, and so on—your transitional obligations would be much higher. In fact, your best bet then might be to announce your organizational intentions in your hook and adopt a different sort of list:

Restaurants
Tourist attractions
Nightlife

As this twist demonstrates, the list approach need not be limited to stories built on enumerations (five of this or the ten best something). Whenever you have a finite number of clearly defined chunks of information or ideas to communicate, structuring your story like a list makes transitions a snap.

Even lists, however, demand a certain logical ordering. Take another look at our round-up of western cities: While a reader might accept a list so completely random in order, an order with more thought behind it would be more pleasing (and, again, easier to write). You don't want to make the reader wonder *why* something comes next, not when it's so easy to impose order on a list.

In this example, you might put the cities in geographical order, from north to south. Or you might organize the story as a mock trip, starting at one geographic extreme and leading the reader across the map (San Antonio, Dallas, Santa Fe, Denver, Reno). You could put the cities in alphabetical order, or in the historical order of their founding. The important thing isn't even that the reader directly perceives your ordering scheme but that there is a scheme, that your list has some intelligence behind it.

You can organize lists according to almost any order you can think of—and all these ways will make the transitions between your elements as easy as writing "To the south . . . ," "Next . . ." or "Second. . . ." Chronology, already discussed at length a few chapters back, is a natural organizing principle, like geography, that leads the reader from one event to the next like the rapt listeners to a campfire storyteller. Similarly, numbers create their own transitions: from largest to smallest, youngest to oldest. Think of the Count on "Sesame Street" or, more grandly, Browning's sonnets: "How do I love thee? Let me count the ways. . . ." No listener to that line will get impatient at transition gaps between the "ways"!

All these organizing principles not only help the reader get from here to there but also aid in understanding your topic. In a list of ideas, for example, you should proceed from the simplest to the most complex. If you help the reader build on what's gone before, you will likewise help make the jump from idea to (more complex) idea.

For instance, what could be simpler than the idea of lists? Doesn't that seem like a good place to start in a list of transition techniques?

The similarity principle

Delving deeper into the structure of your article, a second secret of easy transitions is the principle of similarity. Just as the reader expects one thing after another in a list, so too, he expects like things to follow like. If you're discussing dude ranches, the reader won't be jarred by a transition to another dude ranch, or even to a different type of ranch. On the other hand, jumping from a meditation on the lazy pleasures of the Bar None Old West Dude Ranch to a section on a sophisticated, high-tech nightclub in downtown Dallas is going to take some transitional gymnastics. (Hold that example in your mind till later, though, because it *can* be done.)

If the principle of similarity worked only to make very small transitions (from one steakhouse in a section on restaurants to a different steakhouse, say), it wouldn't be of much use. But think of similarity instead as like a set of children's building toys: Each toy has several ways to link it to another piece. Not *all* the links have to match up, only one. With transitions built on similarity, all you need is one logical link. In describing the historic sites of one of our western cities, for example, you can jump from a church to a whorehouse if they have just one link in common: Were they built the same year? Were they both among the handful of survivors of the great fire of '04? Did a prominent railroad magnate of the era patronize both? The possibilities are endless.

The link of similarity can be as slender as a phrase or an image; it can even be metaphorical. The important thing is to find some seemingly effortless way to lead the reader from A to B on the premise that B is like A in at least one respect.

To see how similarity works in practice, let's go back to my article on Rolls-Royce. At one point in my tour of the operation I wrote:

> . . . Every part is checked by teams of women seated at small tan workbenches, and every gauge used to check every part is checked.
>
> It's a pattern that continues throughout the plant. . . .

The principle of similarity is obvious here: from elaborate quality-control measures in the machine-shop to elaborate quality-control measures elsewhere in the plant.

But similarity can work in less obvious ways as well. In my profile of Malcolm Forbes, for instance, I needed to segue from a description of his posh, collectible-filled office to a section on Forbes's opinions about capitalism and America:

> . . . His mahogany desk is like a miniature of his gallery: jade Fabergé push buttons on the intercom and a gilt writing portfolio with the crowned double monogram of Nicholas and Alexandra. The portfolio contains ideas for Forbes's editorials, two or three of which he dictates every morning.
>
> Malcolm Forbes owns an opinion on almost everything, and he is as happy to share one as he is his more tangible treasures. . . .

Here the similarity is simply of location: the folder and its contents. My little rhetorical flourish about "owning" and "sharing" opinions merely highlighted the connection in the reader's mind and enabled me to move forward with the "sharing" of Forbes's opinions.

Pushing the envelope a bit more, if Forbes's editorials didn't conveniently happen to reside in that antique portfolio, there were other directions the principle of similarity could have let me take the story. Suppose I needed instead to introduce a section about *Forbes* magazine's value to investors: I could have gone from the real-life *portfolio* on the desk to the notion of investment *portfolios*.

That would be merely the transitional trick, of course; if the idea of investments didn't make sense at that point in the overall structure of the story, no amount of wordplay could take the readers there.

Transitions by contrast: On the other hand . . .

A third transition technique, which may seem like mere wordplay, is our old pal contrast. Remember the seemingly impossible transition from old-fashioned dude ranch to high-tech nightspot? Actually, you can build your transition on that very contrast, just as you might with a similarity link:

> If saddle sores and cookouts around the campfire aren't your style, you might prefer the sore dancing feet and gathering around the glittering bar of Dallas's newest nightclub . . .

Contrast would work, too, to make the leap from your historic church to your equally historic (but in a very different way) house of ill repute: "But old Denver had its sinners as well as saints. . . ."

That sentence beginning with "But . . ." (erroneously frowned upon by phalanxes of schoolteachers through the eons) shows how easy and fluid the contrast transition can be. By setting the next idea in opposition to the previous one, you immediately link the two and bring the reader along with you.

This opposition of ideas or subjects goes beyond wordplay. By playing one idea off another, you add to the reader's understanding and advance your article. It's an essential structural "move," a way of assembling the Tinkertoys of your nonfiction:

A
A
But also B
B
But don't forget C . . .

Or, in a structure reminiscent of the "spiral" we examined way back in chapter two:

A
But B
A, however
B, though
But A . . .

Too much of this, obviously, can give the reader a headache. You should be particularly wary of making your story go up and down like a yo-yo without seeming to get anywhere on either the upward or downward swings. If you use the principle of contrast to go from A to (contrasting) B and back to A again, the reader must learn something about A in the process. You have to make the journey through contrasting ideas worthwhile, or soon it simply becomes annoying.

All these techniques—ordered lists, similarity, contrast—are likely to work together in a single article, rather than relying solely on one or the other. You might begin with a list, then use similarity and contrast to ease the move from one item on the list to the next. In our list of western cities, for example, you might liken Hispanic-influenced San Antonio to the old Spanish town of Santa Fe. But you might then contrast historic Santa Fe with the modern gambling strip of Reno.

The effect becomes almost like creating a painting: At some points you want the sky and the sea to merge imperceptibly; at other points, the mountains will only dazzle with their proper glory if set against a sky of a different hue. But all must come together to make one image: The trees in the painting shouldn't look as though they were cut and pasted from another picture by another artist.

Transitions are where all the disparate elements of your article come together into a whole picture, each part bound to the other as if they could not be otherwise. Or, to abruptly switch metaphors, transitions are the grease in the wheels of the roller-coaster you've set your readers in—making sure that, once they start the ride, they don't want to get off until the end.

CHAPTER SEVENTEEN

Endings

A good last impression

I've never been one to worry much about last impressions. I don't polish the backs of my heels, scrutinize the parting glance of my hairdo in the mirror, or fret about wrinkles in the tail of my suitcoat. It's enough of a struggle just making myself presentable for walking *in* the door.

But when it comes to the last impression I leave in an article, I worry. A good ending can pull it all together for a reader, achieving the nonfiction writer's objective of making the whole more than the sum of the assembled parts. (And a bad ending, of course, can ruin all your hard work in leading the reader from there to here.) The right ending can leave the reader with a gasp or a smile, can lock your message in his head with stunning force or near-subliminal subtlety.

Or, as William Zinsser so aptly puts it in *On Writing Well*: "The perfect ending should take the reader slightly by surprise and yet seem exactly right to him. He didn't expect the article to end so soon, or so abruptly, or to say what it said. But he knows it when he sees it. Like a good lead, it works."

And, just as the lead is important for drawing the reader into an article, the ending is vital to the story's ultimate impact. Think of endings in the movies: What if Thelma and Louise had decided instead, what the heck, let's just give ourselves up? What if Charlton Heston hadn't stumbled across the Statue of Liberty at the end of *Planet of the Apes*?

Structurally speaking, your ending is the other side of the bridge that began with your lead, got supported by your hook and takes the reader to—where? It's essential that your ending make the journey seem worthwhile and bring the reader to a satisfactory destination. That destination must deliver on the promise made through your focus, angle and hook. All of which is no mean feat, as the seventeenth-century English clergyman Thomas Fuller noted in *Gnomologia*: "Great is the art of beginning, but greater the art is of ending."

Like the lead, the ending must spring naturally from the heart of your story. A tacked-on ending not only cheats the reader, but leaves a bad taste in the mouth that you have no opportunity to wash out. The ancient Greeks and Romans could get away with *deus ex machina* endings, in which a "god out of a machine" unexpectedly descends to resolve all the story's problems and wrap things up in a tidy package— but not today's writers. Your endings should be as seamless a part of the overall fabric of your article as you can weave.

At least fiction writers and contemporary dramatists have the luxury of crafting events to make a satisfying, integral ending. The trouble with nonfiction is that it's often hard to see exactly where your story ends. In real life, your characters just keep going on and on. If your subject *doesn't* drive off a cliff, you can't write it that way just to whip up a better ending. Stumped by the complexity of fact and duly warned against tacked-on trickery, many nonfiction writers let their articles merely dribble to a close, run on, or stop in an anticlimax.

But endings don't have to put you in a panic. The key to successful endings, not surprisingly, lies in the homework you do before you sit down to write your first words. Just as your outline leads you safely and sanely through your lead, hook, chronology, exposition and other essential elements, so too can advance planning create a safe landing for your article.

As you outline your article and the bits and pieces start to fall into place, you should keep in mind three possible strategies for organizing your ending. These structural secrets—which are not mutually exclusive but may be creatively combined for truly satisfying conclusions— all draw on elements that we've already examined in-depth:

- Finding your ending in your lead
- Finding your ending in your hook
- Finding your ending in your chronology

Let's look at each approach and see how it can take some of the fear and trembling out of finishing what you've started. . . .

Coming full circle

In your lead, you set out a problem, introduced a novel situation, popped a surprise, posed a challenge, asked a question. In your ending, it's only natural to look back to your lead and resolve the problem or answer the question with which you began. Has the situation changed, for better or worse? Was your initial impression accurate? What have you and the readers learned along the way?

Coming full circle in this way can give your nonfiction a pleasing symmetry. Psychologists would add that you are also playing to your audience's powerful built-in desire for *closure*, that sense of waiting for the other shoe to drop.

In a story that offers some new solution to the problems of life, for example, you likely opened by dramatizing the problem. Whether you're tackling household clutter, depression, the challenges of traveling with kids, zits, or sexual dysfunction, the point of your piece is to lead the reader down some possible avenue of help. At the end of the road, it's not surprising that you should wind up back where you started—but with the problem solved.

In a story I wrote for *Link-Up* about help for harried chefs now available online by computer, I opened with a problem straight out of sitcoms:

> Same old story, new happy ending. The boss is coming over for supper and all you have in the house is boring old steak. How do you show that your taste in food is as good as your taste in bosses?
>
> You can solve this "food-processing" problem the same way you'd solve a word-processing dilemma at the office: with your computer. . . .

From there I led readers through the various online options for cooking help. Toward the conclusion of the article, I segued into a section about other gourmet information available online, such as electronic restaurant guides. That made my ending a snap to write: "So if all else fails, take the boss to a restaurant."

That was it—no complicated lead-up or convoluted retracing back to the start. The article was brief enough that the initial problem would still be fresh in the reader's mind; I just had to put a light but logical twist on it.

A similar strategy gave me the ending for an *Easy Living* magazine article that sought to sort out all those "Places Rated" guides to finding the good life. I opened with a real-life first-person experience with those guides:

> I was considering a career move to Dubuque, Iowa, and what kept coming to mind was *New Yorker* editor Harold Ross's comment that his magazine would "not be edited for the little old lady in Dubuque."
>
> I began wading through a sea of studies and statistics, anyway, and soon learned. . . .

The bottom line of my anecdote was that, although Dubuque didn't have much to recommend it statistically, it turned out to be a great place to live—for my family, if not for Harold Ross—thanks to factors numbers can't measure. The quality of life, I pointed out, depends on who's living it.

I developed that theme throughout the article, showing how to make sense of the conflicting data and why, ultimately, you should take the whole rating-places game with a grain of salt. I headed toward the finish with a quote from an expert who supported the notion from my lead: "It's necessary to make value judgments, even if the data are accurate. How do you weigh these factors? Crime rates are higher in New York. Is that offset by the cultural amenities?"

Sharp-eyed readers will note that my expert even thoughtfully brought the comparison back to editor Ross's New York (I had certainly noticed it, and marked it in my outline with a "NY > NY" scribble). So I closed the loop:

> Before you can answer, you must know yourself. Once you've completed that self-examination, you may find paradise in a place you never dreamed of. Sorry—Dubuque's taken.

In articles like these with a light tone, the ending works almost as a punch line. The result, when properly told, can be just as pleasing—and memorable—as a good joke.

But the full-circle approach can also add impact when you want to be taken seriously. By bringing your story 'round again to the start, you can give a sense of completeness to a scene, re-enforce an opening image, or add a twist of irony.

In a profile of Minnesota Fats for the *Philadelphia Inquirer Magazine*, for example, staff reporter Donna St. George began with a scene of the famed pool hustler outside the Hermitage Hotel in Nashville, feeding the birds—hardly the setting you'd expect for the original of *The Hustler*. But the surprise is precisely the point, of course, and St. George begins her narrative in earnest with this lovely spin:

> "Whaddya say, fatty?" he asks a plump bird.
> The question echoes back to him. . . .

After following Fats through his day and, in flashback, through his career, St. George closes with him in the car, heading "home" to the hotel. Fats remembers that the hotel hosted a luncheon that day and that he collected several laundry bags of leftover bread and rice for the birds: " 'They're going to feast tomorrow,' he says happily, 'beyond compare.' " Then Minnesota Fats walks across the street to the marbled lobby of the Hermitage Hotel—"and the street is quiet, no sign of even one pigeon."

Even without the metaphorical fillip—hustlers, after all, make their living from "pigeons"—the sense of coming full circle lends a power and weight to the story.

Answering the question in your hook

Finding your ending in your hook works almost exactly the same as coming full-circle back to your lead. Building an ending off your hook requires only a realization that your hook posed a question or made a promise to the reader; to turn that into an ending, you need only answer the question or deliver on the promise.

Consider the kinds of questions that might form the foundation for an article's hook: Can computers in the classroom ever replace teachers? Did the celebrity fall from grace because his career grew too far too fast, or does the blame lie with his agents and managers? Is there really such a thing as love at first sight? The writer's obligation is to satisfactorily answer that question for the reader by the time the story ends; if the ending itself forms or sums up the answer, so much the better.

For instance, a story answering the question, "Can computers in the classroom ever replace teachers?" might build to a quote (always an effective tool to end an article) from a teacher whose credibility you've already established:

> "Sure, computers can help kids learn," Smith says, surveying the rows of blinking screens in her classroom, "but I'd take a good teacher without computers over a poor one with computers, every time."

That's it. End it. You've presented the pros and cons, the facts and figures and competing points of view. You've found a quote (or it might be an anecdote or some telling detail or scene) that perfectly encapsulates your bottom-line answer to the question encapsulated in your hook. Look (and write) no further—you've got yourself an ending.

Similarly, a profile ought to have a focus that gives it a greater reason for being than just "Meet so-and-so." Powerful profiles may probe the subject's character, asking a fundamental question (expressed most clearly in the hook) whose answer becomes the substance of the article. The profile's conclusion, then, begs for some sort of summation of that answer. You the author can do it, but it's more effective to cast it in the subject's own words or actions. This closing bit can be subtle, even symbolic.

Suppose, for instance, that your profile of the burned-out celebrity posed the question, in the hook, of who was really in charge of his career. The answer that your article develops is that over-eager, greedy agents and managers were really responsible for the star's meteoric rise and fall. If then in your research you were lucky enough to get this little scene, you'd have a ready-made ending:

> A knock on the door signals that the ex-teen idol's time for talking is up. He manages a parting flash of that famous smile, then climbs into a waiting cherry-red Corvette to make his big entrance for the auto show.

The drive onto the auditorium floor is only a few hundred feet. But this time, at least, he's the one in the driver's seat.

That probably seems contrived after the fact, but if you had your focus firmly in mind, at some point the aptness of that scene would leap out at you. It's a bit of business that you could have left out. Or you could have used it without wringing any symbolic import from the scene. But the nonfiction writer alert to nuances of structure and flow would spot the scene as a perfect echo to the hook, and write it to signal the reader that the question posed early on has been answered.

Finding the cut-off

Our made-up closing scene with the ex-teen idol happened also to be at the chronological end of our made-up story. And that's certainly one way chronology can help you find your article's conclusion: End it where the story ends. The interview is over, the race is won, the patient comes out of her coma. Some nonfiction stories come with endings as obvious as those of fiction.

Other articles, alas, are not so neat. The problem may not be solved, the scientists' work goes on, the debate continues.

Still other articles—and this may be the most common situation you'll face—have natural chronological endings, but you must agonize over whether this is indeed the best place for your writing to end. Think of a travel article, for example: You could end almost every travel piece with getting on the plane to go home, with one last look at the lovely island or sparkling city from the air before clouds and distance sweep it into memory. But is that really the best way to end a travel article? *Every* travel article?

You can build your endings on chronology, but you don't have to limit yourself to chronological endings. It's more important for your ending to reflect your focus and angle than the clock or the calendar. Part of your task as a writer is to select the cut-off point for your own work: Should it end with you getting on the plane or with the scene the evening before, sipping a tropical drink while watching the sun go down? If the focus of your article is on the island as the ultimate place to get away from it all, go with the sunset.

Think of the Minnesota Fats example we looked at when considering coming full-circle. Donna St. George chose to end her account with

Minnesota Fats crossing the street to the hotel lobby. She could have followed him into the hotel, or shown him at breakfast the next day, or even stuck with him until he boarded a plane for the next town. But she chose instead the cut-off point that worked most powerfully for her story.

Given that you the writer have the ultimate control over the presentation and selection, how then can you use chronology to help find your endings? The key is finding a cut-off point that has more than merely chronological importance, an ending that resonates with the reader and that reflects your angle and focus.

To pick this cutoff, you might try sketching key points in your chronology in a rough outline:

A. Historical background of Bora-Bora
B. Arrive on Bora-Bora
C. Spectacular island views
D. Encountering the charming people
. . .
M. Tropical sunset
N. Goodbye to the island

Of course, for dramatic effect you would probably write it more like this:

B. Arrive on Bora-Bora
C. Spectacular island views
A. Historical background of Bora-Bora
D. Encountering the charming people
. . .

And so on, flashing back to the historical background only after you've caught the reader's interest.

So where's the best spot to chop off this chain of events? We've already agreed that the tropical sunset makes a better cut-off point than the flight home. But you don't need to be bound by A-B-C chronological order in your endings any more than in your leads. Suppose that your focus is something like, "The people of Bora-Bora turn out to be more beautiful, in their kindness and respect for tradition, than their lovely island." Then you might prefer to extract part of D. "Encountering the charming people" (let's call this second anecdote or whatever, D2) and save it for the ending.

Your actual outline might then look like this:

B. Arrive on Bora-Bora

C. Spectacular island views

A. Historical background of Bora-Bora

D. Encountering the charming people

. . .

M. Tropical sunset

D2. Final remembered encounter with the charming people

While a lengthy chronological twist, such as a full-bore flashback, would be confusing at the end (and violate the one-flashback rule), you could introduce this brief detour as a remembrance:

The gentle splash of the waves in the sunset reminded me of the soft laughter of two little native girls I met the day before . . .

(anecdote)

. . . More so even than the beauty of the sunsets, their smiles, and those of the other Bora-Borans I met, are what will draw me back to this enchanted place.

You can certainly write less labored endings than I can make up here (although now at least I can take that trip to Bora-Bora off my taxes . . .). The point is that you should consider your whole chain of events as you seek for the perfect ending. Finding your ending may be as simple as stopping where the story stops, or it may require a last little backtrack.

Your chronology, like your lead and your hook, should feed into your ending until it seems—to the reader, at least—as perfect and inevitable, yet surprising, as a tropical sunset. When you and the reader arrive there together, you'll know that, yes, this is the place to stop.

Just as this, of course, is the place to end this chapter.

Part Three

PUTTING THE PIECES TOGETHER

CHAPTER EIGHTEEN

Structuring the Profile

Taking the fear out of profile writing

In this third section, we're going to be putting the theory and strategies of parts one and two to work. (Quiet down, those of you in the back murmuring "About time!" You wouldn't expect a show-and-tell on building a house until after a few lessons on using a hammer and drawing blueprints, would you?) This and following chapters will show, by example, how an understanding of structure and flow can help you write some of the most common forms of nonfiction.

You might be surprised, however, that I've chosen to start the parade of examples with a chapter on writing the profile. To many nonfiction writers, the profile—attempting to capture the essence of a personality, often a well-known personality, in a few thousand words on paper—seems the most daunting of assignments. Give them a nice, safe travel story to write instead—a subject without any feelings to interpret, or hurt, a subject you can get your arms around. As an editor, I'll often push writers to come up with profiles, only to have them hand in run-of-the-mill trend stories covered with a thin layer of personality. Profiles can be hard, scary, frustrating.

Which of course is the perfect reason to start with the profile. If a mastery of structure and flow can make writing the personality profile a snap, the rest of the nonfiction panorama must be duck soup.

But that's not the only reason to start with the profile. The fact is, I've never found profiles daunting to write—for reasons that go to the heart of a good profile's structure and flow.

Remember the importance of finding your focus? Well, the good news about the profile is that your focus is narrowed before you even begin: Your story is going to be about John Doe or Jane Smith. That's a good head start on a focus, much better than launching into a story about "child care" or "buying a car" or some similarly nebulous topic.

What's more, you probably start off with a pretty clear idea of what makes John Doe or Jane Smith worth reading (and writing) about. If your John Doe is the multi-zillionaire head of a revolutionary software company, your focus is likely going to include Doe's riches and how he got them. If Jane Smith is the first woman to own an NBA franchise, you will almost certainly focus on the contrast between Smith as a woman and the men's-club atmosphere of the NBA.

That's not all there is to it, naturally, or magazines would be awash in wonderful profiles. You still need to decide what angle you'll take on all those givens. Ideally, you'll find something surprising that gives your profile a special zing (maybe Doe, the software king, really wanted to be a pro basketball player). The best profiles not only show readers about an interesting individual; they reveal something about what makes that person tick.

What makes 'em tick?

I found a literal answer, of sorts, to that question of "What makes 'em tick?" in a profile of Commodore Grace Murray Hopper, then the Navy's oldest active-duty officer, that I wrote for *American Way* magazine some years back. The Hopper profile is one of my favorites—perhaps because the Commodore, who died not long ago, was such an American original. It's hard to go wrong with such great material, and my story wound up not only being bought by *American Way* but also reprinted in a reading textbook.

Having great material can be a curse, however, without a strong structure to pull it all together. Otherwise, awash in good quotes and telling anecdotes, you can find yourself paralyzed: What goes first? How can you leave anything out? How does all this great stuff fit together?

Hopper, who'd already been interviewed by Morley Safer for *60*

Minutes before I profiled her, was a fount of quotes and anecdotes—the sort of personality who makes great television. In order to make a great profile out of her, I had to narrow in on some focus beyond her simple celebrity. I had to structure the quotes and anecdotes to say something about what made her tick.

I found my focus, as I said, in a literal ticking—of a clock in Hopper's office. This particular clock ran backward. Why? So, Hopper explained, no one in her office can say, "We've always done it this way."

That would be my take on Commodore Grace Murray Hopper: a woman who has gone against the conventional wisdom. That clock, too, would help form the organizing metaphor of my profile of a woman whose favorite stock prop was another time-related object: a wire 11.8 inches long, the distance electricity can travel in a nanosecond (a billionth of a second). Clocks, nanoseconds, the *oldest* (another question of time) officer in the Navy . . . I could see a structure coming together.

Useful structures, those that are true to their story, often spring like this from the subject itself. Given the chance to percolate on what's truly memorable and important about a story, your subconscious brain will begin to make the connections that ultimately become your writing blueprint. The links may be literal, chronological, metaphorical, or a combination of these and other strands. Where you want them to lead is this: A sense of exactly what story you are going to tell (your focus) and how you are going to tell it (your structure).

Your focus, then, becomes the heart of your story. Your structure unfolds into the outline that takes this focus out of your brain and into the reader's.

My focus, once I hit upon the backward-running clock and what that seemed to say about my subject, couldn't have been more clear. It found specific expression in my hook, which came in my second paragraph:

> Hopper has been doing things her own way for most of her 78 years—long enough to make her the Navy's oldest officer on active duty. When computers were but a twinkle in the eyes of a few mathematicians, she turned the fundamental problems upside-down and solved some of the toughest. . . .

There you have it, in just two sentences, all the essential elements of my story: doing it her own way . . . the Navy's oldest officer on active duty . . . a computer pioneer . . . solving problems by turning them upside-down. . . . Now all I had to do was build a story that would substantiate and illustrate those points.

Picking your story's girders

Fortunately, I had this whole notion of clocks and time with which to form girders for my story. With that in mind, I broke the story into four sections, each with a clock or time aspect at its start:

1. *A short introductory section, containing the lead and the hook:* The clock in her office as a symbol of how she's been doing it her own way for a long career. What about that career makes her noteworthy. How her career and her character intersect.

2. *A longer section, built on chronology:* As a little girl, Hopper used to take apart the family's alarm clocks. How her against-the-grain career as a woman in mathematics began and blossomed. Her opinions about feminism and women in computing.

3. *The longest section by far, weaving together her opinions and anecdotes:* The "nanosecond" as a symbol of the fast-moving computer revolution she helped to start. Her opinions and predictions about the computer age.

4. *A short closing section, picking up the chronology from section 2 and bringing us back to now:* How the "clock" ran out on Hopper's career, with retirement. How she came back out to active duty for a second, much-celebrated career, from which she has no plans to retire (pointing toward the future, always a good ending strategy).

The clocks-and-time thread woven through my rough outline not only gave me a sense that the story would hold together; it also laid the groundwork for smoother transitions in the actual writing of the first draft. For readers, it gave the story a resonance beyond a mere recitation of Hopper's resume.

From this bare-bones, four-part plan, I built a detailed outline into which I plugged specific references to my notes. The final outline took up one side of a sheet from a yellow legal pad, a thicket of blue pen scrawls punctuated by red notebook-page numbers. Abbreviations ran throughout: "p" for people, "cp" for computers, "H" for Hopper.

Arrows indicated inserts and on-second-thought rearrangements of whole chunks of material. To anyone else, it would likely be undecipherable; to me, however, it was the essential plan for writing my first draft. With this outline behind me I knew that the actual writing would be a breeze—the hardest work was done. What I had on this single piece of paper was like a dehydrated version of my story; getting to the first draft would be like just adding water.

Rehydrating the outline

Let's look at the actual building of some parts of that "dehydrated story" to see how all the challenges of structure and flow come together and, by and large, get solved in something as simple and scrawled as my outline.

The lead was easy. As soon as I hit upon the backward-running clock, I knew it would open my article. It offered a sense of surprise, while at the same time nicely encapsulating my theme of what makes Hopper tick.

In my outline, the whole first paragraph was represented simply by:

> Clock in office

I knew, without having to spell it out, exactly what I was going to do with that clock in her office. Here's how the finished article began:

> The clock in the Pentagon office of Commodore Grace Murray Hopper, U.S. Navy Reserve, runs backwards. It tells perfectly good time, nonetheless, Hopper explains to the curious: "That's so nobody in the office can say, 'We've always done it this way.'"

That was a good way of grabbing readers' attention, besides what it did for my theme, but I knew I couldn't count on all readers already being familiar with—and interested in—my subject, despite her relative celebrity. So I opted to head straight for the hook from my lead (particularly since my hook built naturally on the contrariness exemplified in the lead). My outline from there was a bit more detailed (and each point, of course, had one or more attached notebook page references, which I'll spare you):

> Been doing it her own way
> Oldest active officer
> Solved some of toughest computer problems—turning upside-

down

> On lecture tours: What ships are built for

This last point formed the conclusion of my hook paragraph—and also the anchor, if you will, for my ending (as we'll see). In the article it became:

> . . . As she tells audiences on her whirlwind lecture tours, "I have a piece of important advice for you: Do it. You'll find on many, many occasions it's much easier to apologize than it is to get permission. One of my mottos is: 'A ship in port is safe, but that is not what ships are built for.'"

The rest of the outline for section A was mostly scene-setting, giving the reader a visual sense of this intriguing person and playing off the language in the hook:

> As steely & patrician as battleship herself—describe
> Gleaming insignia—recent promotion

Those two points turned into this nautical paragraph:

> Commodore Grace Murray Hopper looks as steely and patrician as a battleship herself, red medals flying against her dark dress uniform and hair white as froth under the prow of her cap. She's the sort of officer who'd be spit 'n' polished anyway, but the single star of her commodore's insignia gleams particularly brightly—sign of a recent promotion after a celebrated career as Captain Hopper.

I'd set out my theme, introduced my subject and spelled out why readers should care about her, linked the lead to my overall focus (with another telling quote that I knew I'd come back to, for another resonant note, in the ending), delivered a bit of description, and updated readers on the latest development in her career—all in three paragraphs. Note, too, how my outline gave me a clear path to transitions between those paragraphs—particularly important when working to draw the reader in with the opening. Look at the last line of each paragraph and see how the first line of the next plays off of it.

But now it was time to launch into section B, jumping way back in the chronology to Hopper's first interest in gadgets. This transition had to be smooth, too, lest readers get lost between sections. Because I knew I'd be mentioning Hopper's recent promotion, I could plan this wordplay in my outline, before the actual words got on paper:

> When H rank Little Girl, take apart clocks

Which became, as I knew it would:

> When Hopper's rank was merely Little Girl, she used to take apart the family's clocks to see what made them tick. . . .

From there, mixing quotes and narration, I traced Hopper's career, how she got sidetracked by her gender from her original ambition to be an engineer, her study of mathematics and entry into the Navy. At this point, I planned a minor digression:

> Joined Navy '43—grtgrfather
> But no use for feminism
> "Man of the Year," "chair"
> women superior programmers
> GMH her own best example
> Building Mark I computer . . .

Here I've indented the detour so it stands out, though my actual outline wasn't so tidy. The digression—covering Hopper's views on feminism, her willingness to accept "Man of the Year" awards, her distaste for such de-genderized terms as "chair," and her argument that women excel in computer programming—came here because I knew I had a natural way into it, an ideal setup quote linked to Hopper following her great-grandfather ("grtgrfather" in my outline) into the Navy:

> ". . . When I was commissioned I got a big sheaf of spring flowers, took them out to his grave and told him it was all right for a woman to be a naval officer. Otherwise he'd roll over in his grave."

Contrast, then, let me move smoothly into her contrary views on feminism: "Though Hopper is still a single career woman, as liberated as they come, she plainly has no use for feminism. . . ."

When you plan a digression, it's equally important to plan a way *back* into your main storyline. Here, I knew that after my chunk on Hopper's views about women as programmers I could easily slide back into her career chronology—talking about her own stellar career as a programmer.

From that sub-section, I planned a transition into section C of my overall plan using the next of my time-themed elements—Hopper's sheaf of "nanoseconds":

> Unlike the backwards clock in her office, the computer revolution Hopper helped wind up has been racing forwards. The Mark I, a 58-foot behemoth of vacuum tubes, could add three numbers a second. Today's microchip marvels do the same work in a nanosecond—a billionth of a second.
>
> The nanosecond is a stock prop of Hopper's lectures. . . .

That reference to the backward clock of the lead not only reemphasized my theme; it served as a subtle signal to readers that here I was beginning a fresh section—a new lead, almost.

Section C consisted of just over a dozen points worth making about Hopper and computers, all gathered together for clarity and organized to flow smoothly from one into another. Here, too, a simple chronology reigned: Hopper's comments about today's computers came first, followed by her predictions about the future, then her thoughts on how people are adapting (or failing to adapt) to the rapid pace of technological change. This section moved to its conclusion with her thoughts on young people's eagerness to embrace the computer revolution:

> young people—easy, greatest natural resource

But now I needed a way to turn the focus back on Hopper herself, preferably something that emphasized my focus on her willingness to go against the grain. I seized on an anecdote about Hopper's own crew of young (see the transition ahead, linked to her views on other young people?) Navy programmers:

> when her crew of young programmers not enough respect— take off uniforms, business cards

This outline note became:

> When the so-called experts didn't properly respect her own crew of young Navy programmers, she hit upon a typically Hopper solution: She had them take off their uniforms—that was

the hard part. Then she paid for business cards for every young programmer, giving each one the title of "manager."

I balanced this with a chunk on how Hopper's crew returns the respect and affection (calling her "Grandma," but never to her face). Section C ended with a Navy veteran who served under her: "She's the best commander I ever had."

This set up my concluding section, D, which I introduced with one more reference to the clocks theme:

> But the clock seemingly ran out on Grace Murray Hopper's career shortly after her 60th birthday—the saddest day of her life. She retired.

The final five paragraphs got her back out of retirement and on the road to *60 Minutes*-level celebrity. I wove in her reaction to her fame and then closed with her vow not to retire again. Here I picked up on the quote I used in my hook paragraph. In the outline it read:

> Not retire 2nd time—not what ships built for

Which, after "adding water," turned into this carefully prepared-for ending:

> The Navy's oldest active officer adds that she harbors no thoughts of retiring a second time. That is not what ships are built for.

Knowing long before I got there that this would be my ending gave me a great feeling of confidence in writing through the first draft. Would a ship, after all, leave harbor without knowing its destination?

Eight pointers for better profiles

You can apply these same tactics and techniques to structuring your own profiles, making the profile as un-daunting an exercise as anything you'll tackle in nonfiction. Thinking through your profile's structure and flow, binding it to a tightly focused angle, not only makes it easier to write but also imbues it with a power and impact that leaves readers with a sense of revelation. The properly structured profile tells readers something fresh about even a familiar subject. It's more than just a string of colorful quotes and anecdotes.

Here are some tips to keep in mind as you sit down to structure your own profiles:

1. *Find your angle—preferably, some sense of what makes your subject tick—and build your structure to support it.* Resist the temptation to include material that's merely colorful but that doesn't fit your focus. The most colorful, quotable subjects demand the most rigorous structures; you're trying to craft a verbal ballet, not unleash a three-ring circus. Of course, the sooner you start this process—even before your primary interview, if possible—the better (and the easier it will be!).

2. *The most useful structural "girders" spring from within the story itself.* Look for themes, metaphors and images in your material that can help glue it together. A great part of the nonfiction writer's artistry comes in spotting and developing these patterns that make a whole of seemingly disparate parts.

3. *Look for ways to use your structure to weave together the three most important parts of your profile: the lead, the hook and the ending.* When each of these essential parts supports and resonates with the other, you have the start of a profile that will come together as a whole in the reader's mind. You'll also have an article that will be much easier to outline and write!

4. *When in doubt, fall back on some variation of the "Middle Column" approach seen back in chapter two.* Though my four-part Hopper profile may not at first seem like a variation on this basic structure, stripped of its bells and whistles it starts to look mighty familiar:

1. Grabber lead, often using contrast or the collision of opposites (the backward clock)
2. Hook, setting the specific of the lead in a general context, establishing the basis for the reader's interest, and articulating the angle (doing things her own way, etc.)
3. Background and development of the hook (brief description of Hopper)
4. Chronological beginning of the story (chronology of Hopper's career from her childhood fascination with gadgets)
5. Chronology up to and through the dramatic lead (Hopper's Navy career, with comments on feminism)
6. Completing chronology, weaving in remaining exposition neces-

sary to support the story's premise (Hopper in her prime, with exposition on computers; her retirement and second career)

7. Dramatically satisfying end ("not what ships are built for")

5. Build your outline with broad strokes first, then flesh out subsidiary points. In my Hopper example, I started by developing four main sections, then filled in what logically fell under each broad part of the profile. Breaking the organizational challenge down into smaller challenges (*OK, I have all the computer stuff together—now what order should these points go in?*) lets you concentrate on one set of problems at a time.

6. As you fill out your outline, plan your transitions. It's much easier to solve your transitional dilemmas now, before you've written a word, than to try to retrofit solutions onto existing paragraphs. And having preplanned transitions makes the actual writing of your profile much smoother and less stressful. Plan transitions between sections as well as between paragraphs; even if you expect to rely on simply an extra line of space between major sections of your profile, you must plan how each section will end, how the next will begin, and the relationship between the two. Effortless transitions are particularly important in profiles, where you are seeking to create a sense of wholeness out of the jangly reality of an individual's life and work.

7. Plan entries—and exits!—for any digressions from the main narrative. It goes without saying that these "digressions" are structural only, not material that falls outside your focus. In profiling a person, you will often want to plan places to elaborate on some aspect of that person's career or on something that emerges from an interview—supporting evidence for your fundamental thesis. Make sure that your outline shows not only how you will dip into these elaborations but also how you will climb back out.

8. Know where your profile will end before you set out to get there. Don't forget that a profile, no less than a chronological narrative, is a journey on which you and the reader embark together. You must be the guide, and at journey's end the reader must feel the trip was worthwhile. No guide worth his salt would set out with a map that had no destination!

Keeping these principles in mind will not only help you write better profiles, but other varieties of nonfiction as well. Think about how often the popular forms of nonfiction really resemble profiles: A travel piece, for example, can be considered a profile of a place, rather than a person, and structured much the same way (anecdotal lead . . . hook . . . chronology of the place . . . the place today . . .). Many trend articles come down to a "profile" of the trend, seeking to show what it is and what makes it tick much as you would explore a person's life and career.

Understanding what makes a profile "tick," in other words, will go a long way toward making all your nonfiction go like clockwork.

CHAPTER NINETEEN

Trend and Service Stories

Sifting through story decisions

In one sense, the profile is the easiest of the standard repertoire of magazine articles to get your arms around, structurewise. As we saw in the previous chapter, for all its complexities the profile at least comes with a head start on your focus. Other magazine articles—trend stories, service pieces—begin much more open-ended, placing a heavier burden on the writer to narrow and define the focus.

Think about it. Let's say you set out to tackle an article on new trends in cars. (Put more of a service spin on the same subject, and it could be a buyer's guide to what's new in cars.) So far your focus consists of two concepts: "new" and "cars." Both ideas will need a lot of angling before you're ready to structure an article.

Take "what's new," for starters. Are you going to cover just new technology, or will your piece also extend to new styling and luxury features? What about safety devices? Will you discuss just what's new in the latest model year, or do you plan to survey the unfolding of new automotive technology over the past, say, five years?

Even the topic of "cars" isn't as simple as it seems. Should your article cover all types of cars or only sedans? What about trucks, sport-utility vehicles and convertibles? And does it make sense to include top-of-the-line luxury models such as Jaguar and Rolls-Royce, even though your average reader can't afford them?

Decisions, decisions—but this is the essence of the trend or service story. You must slice a small but compelling piece out of all there is to know and package it in a way that communicates one or two clear ideas to the reader. It's not unlike building a sand castle in the world's largest beach, using only sand of a certain color.

Much of your sand-sifting must already be done long before you get to actually outlining your article, of course (if not, it's back to chapter one for you!). But even the most rigorously focused writer will usually still come to the point of structuring an article with enough "good stuff" for a dozen trend and service pieces. How do you write just one—and the right one?

That feeling of cramming thirty pounds of material into a five-pound bag is endemic to trend and service pieces. However many words you're assigned, it's never enough.

That's why, for this chapter, I thought I'd dissect the structure of a particularly short article—just 1,200 words—with a big topic: a trend story (with, as you'll see, some reader-service elements blended in) I wrote for *Friendly Exchange* magazine about "virtual reality" and travel. It shows how you can cover a lot of ground in a very few words, while at the same time imparting plenty of information—the essence, in short, of a successful trend or service story.

Creating an article by categories

"Virtual reality," of course, is one of those trendy terms that has come to mean everything and nothing. By comparison, our imaginary dilemma about "what's new in cars" seems a snap. "Virtual reality" could encompass anything from high-tech headsets to those big-screen movies in science museums, from flight simulators costing millions to games on home computer screens.

Nor did the "travel" component help me narrow it down much. The editor's idea was that virtual reality can now take you to the bottom of the sea or inside an atom, without getting wet or shrinking. Beyond that general notion of "virtual travel," I wanted to slant the article toward technologies that more specifically simulated real-world travel: virtual plane flights, car rides and even space voyages. Once I got into researching the story, I filtered in the notion of virtual reality *at* popular travel destinations—specifically, theme parks and museums. My ideal example became a virtual journey (a simulated submarine ride, a high-tech magic-carpet flight) *at* a travel destination (a new nautical museum, Walt Disney World, Las Vegas). Other examples would circle around this goal, fitting into my article or falling out depending on how closely they matched or helped illuminate it.

Remember, I had to accomplish all this in just 1,200 words. Plus I had to give some background and explanation of what virtual reality is and why this is now a trend accessible to the general public. And of course I wanted to end with some ideas about where "virtual travel" might go from here.

As I did my research, with this focus in mind, several broad categories of "virtual travel" began to emerge. Categorization is one of the essential tools for building a trend/service piece: You and the reader have a lot of ground to cover, and it will go better for all concerned if you can break up the big picture into component parts. Your article on what's new in cars, for instance, might form into categories on what's new under the hood, trends in exterior styling, innovations in safety, and new gadgets and gizmos inside the passenger compartment. Whether you break out these categories with subheads or "bullets" or simply use them to help cluster your material, they can make a complex topic more manageable.

In this case, I identified four main types of technology that might be considered "virtual travel":

1. Attractions that were essentially video games offering greater immersion in the game, such as a tank-battle simulation.

2. Attractions that were souped-up movies with the addition of motion, such as seats that move with the on-screen action. These included a theme-park ride that put you in the driver's seat of the race-car movie *Days of Thunder*, as well as a film that took viewers on a joyride through the telephone system.

3. True, total-immersion technology that approached the "holosimulations of the *Star Trek* series. Here I put a virtual voyage to the bottom of the sea at a new nautical museum, as well as a new *Indiana Jones* attraction at Walt Disney World.

4. Examples of virtual reality used for more artistic ends, such as exhibits that transport visitors to wartorn Yugoslavia or the Canadian Rockies.

Each category was defined by two factors: level of technology (in the sense of its ability to create virtual realism) and purpose (competitive play, thrill ride, art). In general, I ordered the categories from lowest to highest technology and (making a value judgment here) from lowest to highest purpose—from juiced-up video games to museum-level art.

In addition to these four main "buckets" of information, I wanted to point the reader toward the future of "virtual travel" and bring this technology from the museum or theme park closer to home. This would not account for much of my 1,200 words, but it did seem to demand an additional mini-category:

> Virtual travel comes home, using helmets and headgear that put the user into a home computer-generated environment.

That gave me five categories I needed to plug into my structure. I knew I'd also need these essential components, roughly in this order:

1. A lead
2. A hook, including a non-technical definition of virtual reality
3. An explanation of why this trend is taking off now
4. A hint of where this trend might ultimately lead

With only 1,200 words to work with and five categories plus four article elements to cover, I knew I'd be boiling down pretty furiously as I outlined and even as I wrote my first draft. But thinking about the challenge in this way helped me face it more fearlessly. In coming up with my categories and enumerating my storytelling chores, moreover, I threw out plenty of otherwise interesting material that—thanks to this process—I could see simply didn't fit into my story. Finally, this planning also gave me a clear sense of how much I could afford to tell about each category: With only a couple of hundred words, at most, to spend on even the biggest subtopic, I had a good feel for how much I could put into my outline and how much (lots!) I'd have to leave out.

Making it mesh

Once I'd assembled all the pieces of my structure in this way, it was time to formally organize them into an outline (if you can call scribbles on a legal pad "formal'). Because each set of categories or story elements carried with it a logical internal order, outlining mostly meant ordering and meshing these three groups of "stuff": four main categories, one mini-category, four story elements.

Much of this was easy. I had already planned the home chunk as a follow-up from my four main categories, so naturally it went after the big four. The fifth story element—a planned ending pointing forward into the future—fell logically thereafter.

That left, as crucial issues, where to attach my four main categories (and all that now hung from them) to the rest of my story elements, and how the main categories connected, in particular, with my lead and grab-the-reader examples.

I might, for instance, have chosen to lead with a striking example from category one. Next, a hook paragraph would set the lead in context and explain why the reader should care about "virtual travel." Then examples from categories two, three and four would tease the reader further before I delved into the background and explained virtual reality. This structure would nicely prepare readers for the more detailed sections on categories one, two, three and four that would then follow.

Taking a different tack, I could have opened with an example from category four—"virtual travel" at its highest and most impressive, according to my order of things. Then would follow the hook, the background, and categories one through four, bringing the order of things back to the lead, almost in the manner of *in medias res*.

Because of the slippery nature of my subject, however, I decided instead to lead with the clearest, most definitive example of "virtual travel," real or fictional, that I could come up with:

> The recent movie *Star Trek: Generations* opens with Captain Picard and crew sailing over the ocean blue in a scene right out of *H.M.S. Pinafore*—all simulated by the Starship Enterprise's "holodeck." Even in the 24th century, it seems, folks will still want to get away from it all.

That idea of the "holodeck" seemed to me (and to my editor, who referred to it in her original assignment letter) to capture most vividly and concisely the far-out concept that my article would be aiming toward. It was cleaner and less cluttered and took less explanation than any of my nonfictional examples from theme parks or museums.

It also made a smooth lead-in to my hook, which said in essence:

"Holodecks" that will take you on similarly incredible journeys may be a reality sooner than you think. Here's how the article actually continued:

> But holodecks may be less science-fictional than most of *Star Trek*. Virtual reality—as seen in *Star Trek* and movies such as *The Lawnmower Man*—is already making it possible to travel to Mars or the bottom of the sea, to drive coast-to-coast without leaving the arcade or to follow an electron through the wireways of the phone system. Though you can't yet walk a simulated plank and get wet, as in *Star Trek: Generations*, you can take virtual voyages so vivid that the weak-of-stomach may prefer to travel with their eyes closed.

Unfortunately, though this hook was mighty effective, its claims were so strong that I didn't feel I could go on without some specific examples to back it up. Here I might have consciously picked examples from each of my four categories, in order, to mirror the rest of the article ahead. But I decided that the four categories were secondary to the main, gosh-wow thrust of "virtual travel is here!"—my focus, after all, was not on the existence of four categories per se. (In other articles, however, the categories themselves might be not merely a useful organizing device but an essential focus of the story: three competing theories of what killed the dinosaurs, for example, or four "undiscovered" Caribbean island paradises.)

So I followed with three one-paragraph examples, regardless of category, chosen for their color and impact. The third example also gave me a transition to quotes from the virtual-reality scientist/artist who created it, explaining something about these real-world "holodecks." In effect, I created a fifth story element—a section of examples—to complete the work of grabbing the reader, before the rest of my plan unfolded.

Could I have done it otherwise? Sure. But the point is: I made the structure of my story do what I needed done, instead of becoming a prisoner of the categories I'd created.

Putting it all together

The categories still dominated the rest of my outline, which spun out almost on its own once I'd resolved the tricky problems of the opening section. Frankly, knowing that I had the bottom three-quarters of the story pretty well in hand helped me to wrestle through the opening. I knew that if I could just get the story started, it would be all downhill from there.

So here's how the whole article came together, combining my four categories, one mini-category, and now *five* story elements:

Lead
Hook
Examples
Why now

Four main categories (in increasing order of sophistication, technical and artistic):
1. Video games
2. Movies
3. Total immersion
4. Artistic expressions
One mini-category:
Home

Where next?

We've already seen how this outline turned into a successful start to the story. I used the expert's quote at the end of the examples to segue into a brief explanation of why virtual reality is now popping up in theme parks and museums (as the reader had just seen in my examples): ". . . such simulated journeys have become possible for the general public only recently." The reason? "Leaps in computer technology have made simulations possible for theme parks, shopping malls and—soon—even the home. . . ." (Note how here I pointed toward the last of my categories and mini-categories, virtual reality at home.)

From there the writing was straightforward as can be: "This technological revolution is turning consumers into virtual tourists in four main ways: . . ."

After sections describing my four categories and sprinkling in more examples (this time, strictly by category), I planned this transition in my outline: *Not just theme pks & museums—*

Next came the home, which led seamlessly to this closing section of quotes from Vito Sanzone of Iwerks, one of the leaders in virtual-reality attractions:

"In 10 years," predicts Iwerks's Sanzone, "you'll be able to sit at home in your own personal simulator. It's obvious that's coming."

When it does, will anyone still bother with non-virtual travel? "Nothing will replace going to Paris, seeing and smelling the real thing," Sanzone says, then laughs at the thought of "smelling" your destination.

"Well, maybe there is an advantage to doing it in virtual reality."

And that, some 1,200 words after holodecks, was that.

Seven map-making tips

My categorizing and outlining gave me, ultimately, a map that helped me find my way through a bewildering forest of facts and ideas. It helped me see the forest for the trees, to stretch a metaphor, and gave me confidence that I could come out on the other side. When making your own maps for trend and service stories, keep in mind these tips and techniques:

1. *Force yourself to focus as tightly as possible as soon as possible.* The nature of trend and service pieces is more wide-open than the profile, so focus becomes even more critical. You need to decide not only what angle you plan to take on your topic, but how wide a net you're going to cast. "What's new in cars" won't suffice; "what's new this model year in styling and technology for convertibles" might.

2. *When in doubt, throw it out.* You will always have more material for a trend or service article than you will be able to fit in your word count—that's the nature of the beast. Try to develop as clear a test of what fits your focus and what doesn't as you can (like my "ideal example" of virtual travel), so you'll know when something strays too far from that center.

Examine each possible element of your article as dispassionately and ruthlessly as possible. If it's not absolutely essential to what you're working to convey, don't put it in your outline. You can always go back and add it in later, if you come up short (which has happened maybe, what, twice in the whole history of nonfiction writing?).

3. *Use categories to organize your material.* Think of these as buckets into which you pour portions of your material, or piles into which you sort your essential points and facts. The categories per se may wind up in your actual writing ("Six new looks for convertibles are making the scene this year . . .") or may appear only in your outline. Either way, categorization is a valuable tool to start sorting your material into the order in which it might work its way into your first draft. You'll also find some material that doesn't fit into your categories—if so, see tip number two.

Not all categories are created equal. You may find it most useful to organize your material into two main categories plus four smaller "buckets"—that's fine. The point is to go through everything you have to work with, analyze it, and divide it into piles that are easier to organize and relate to one another than one big, undifferentiated pile.

4. *Organize categories and subcategories for logical flow.* Thinking about how one category relates to the next not only helps you put them in a tentative order, but ultimately makes for smoother reading. You might go from small to big, old to new, east to west; the order doesn't matter, but the act of ordering does. You might even combine two ordering principles, as I did to stack up my four main virtual travel categories.

If you have various levels of categorization, you need to determine how the categories and subcategories relate to each other. How do the apples and oranges go together, beyond the fact that they're all fruit? (If you have four new styles of convertibles, for instance, and three new roof materials, do the roofs relate to all four styles or are they a subset available only with style number two?)

5. *Make sure you have all the other essential story elements: lead, hook, background as needed, ending.* Some of these may completely match, or merge into, the categories you've identified. Others may form additional "buckets" of material that lead into and out of your basic categories. Your lead, for example, may be part of one of your categories, an entire category unto itself, or a separate element that (as in my holodecks opening) simply sets the stage for your categories.

6. *The reader is more important than the neatness of your structure.* Sometimes you have to bend and stretch your categories to earn and keep the reader's interest. You may find yourself creating a new cate-

gory or story element, or jettisoning whole categories, in order to keep the story moving and keep it focused.

The more of a service slant that a story takes, generally, the easier you'll find it to get and hold reader interest: That second person ("you") is a recipe for reader involvement. The more abstract and trend-driven your article becomes, the more you'll have to squeeze your structure to win readers (and the more important the hook becomes, as we've already seen).

7. *Build transitions into your outline.* Your "buckets" of material can't stand alone; they need to lead into another category or story element. Smart ordering of your categories can help create transitions, but you also need to note rhetorical tricks and out-of-category logical links that can turn into transitions. If you have five otherwise equal categories and one holds a quote by the same speaker you want to quote in your ending, you might want to put that category last; jumping from speaker X in category five to speaker X in the ending will be easier than if readers have forgotten about speaker X because she was three pages ago.

By building your outline around categories, of course, you've created a number of ready-made transitions. Once you've promised four new looks in convertibles, readers won't be jarred when, after Look Number One, you jump to Look Number Two.

Even with careful categorization, orchestration of story elements and transition planning, you may find yourself scribbling changes in your trend or service article outlines. Arrows mark the shuffle of a category from here to there. Whole categories get crossed out. Even in the actual writing of your first draft, elements may appear and disappear, and the final draft may have several twists and turns never reflected in your outline.

Not to worry. You've tackled a big challenge with a trend story or a service article, attempting to corral some portion of the universe into a few thousand words. If you have to modify your map along the way to better reflect the landscape once you're actually standing there, that's only to be expected—and it's sure better than setting out with no map at all.

CHAPTER TWENTY

Humor and Essays

Why it's harder than it looks

In the past couple of chapters, it seems we have turned the pyramid of the article-writing repertoire on its head in terms of difficulty. We've seen how the profile, which to most nonfiction writers seems the most daunting possible assignment, turns out to be the most easily focused. Trend and service pieces, ostensibly simpler than the profile, present somewhat higher demands on the writer's structural powers.

Humorous pieces and essays, of course, appear to be the easiest forms for the nonfiction writer to tackle. (Ask any magazine editor, swamped by submissions of humor and essays when all the editor really wants is a well-crafted profile or service piece, if you doubt the widespread acceptance of the belief that almost anyone can write humor and essays.) After all, what could be simpler? Without having to do a lot of research and interviewing, you just spin out your thoughts and surely someone will want to read them—right?

Alas, all too wrong. The truth is, of all the pantheon of nonfiction-writing possibilities, humor and essays are the most difficult to structure and the hardest to write in a way that will engage and retain the reader's attention. Since humor and essays can, in effect, be about anything, they often wind up being about nothing. Because these forms spring onto the page without any predefined external focus, because their structural underpinnings are entirely up to the writer, they represent the purest example of the nonfiction writer working without a net. It's like the difference between baking a cake from a mix and whipping one up from scratch—including milling your own flour and snatching the eggs from under the chickens.

As William Zinsser puts it in *On Writing Well*, addressing humor in particular: "Humor is not a separate organism that can survive on its own frail metabolism. It's a special angle of vision granted to certain writers who already write good English."

For our purposes in exploring structure and flow, the problem with these varieties of nonfiction is exactly their wide-open nature. Paradoxically, structure is of the greatest importance when the material itself is the least structured and predefined. The spinning out of an effective essay or humorous article must be as carefully calibrated and planned as the cutting of a diamond—one wrong move and the whole thing can go to pieces.

Finding revelation within your material

All of the strategies we've already seen for structuring an effective nonfiction article apply equally to humor and essays. These forms, too, demand focus and rhythm; conflict and contrast are essential tools here, and flow is a particular challenge. But the secret to successful humor and essays is a special sense of unity, which we explored back in chapter six.

Unity, in the sense of knowing what to put in and what to leave out, is important to humor and essays, since these wide-open genres let you draw upon the whole world, your whole life's experience. Learn what to leave out or you'll quickly leave out the readers.

But beyond that obvious demand for unity is the narrower need for all the parts you do put in to come together to create some sort of revelation. This sense of revelation can be as sharp as the punch line of a joke, or as subtle as the dawning of an inner inspiration.

To see what I mean by "revelation," though, think about the revelation that makes a joke work. An effective joke takes you along a path that seems to be going in one direction, then surprises you with the revelation that in fact you've been led to a completely different and unexpected place. Yet what makes the joke funny rather than just nonsense is that the place revealed by the punch line is not *utterly* unexpected. In the fresh light of the punch line's revelation, you can see that there were clues along the path you thought was heading someplace else. The punch line takes those clues, gives you a surprising way of looking at them, and pulls together all that's gone before into a new—and humorous—whole.

This may sound like a mighty highfalutin' explanation of a phenomenon as basic and familiar as the yarn told at the water cooler or the *Tonight Show* monologue. But it helps to understand what *happens* in a joke, because you want to achieve the same thing—in a much grander fashion, perhaps—in your humor and even in your essays.

Consider this joke that cruelly and unfairly humiliates the noble people of North Dakota (being from *South* Dakota, I know all about making fun of North Dakotans). The lead-up to the punch line starts your mind heading in one direction:

> Two North Dakotans were shoveling snow. One said to the other, "This is too much work. Let's just burn it."

Your reaction on hearing this front-end of the joke is, of course: "What an idiot. Doesn't he know you can't burn snow?" The mental picture that springs to mind is of this poor, stupid fellow futilely attempting to set snow ablaze or of snow, subjected to flames, turning messily into flame-dousing water.

The punch line takes this line of thought and gives it a sharp detour. To the other North Dakotan, the problem with burning snow isn't at all what you might expect:

> "No," replied the other North Dakotan. "What would we do with the ashes?"

Though this twist is surprising—and funny—it is not as unexpected as it might seem. You have already been prepared for the notion that these are two mighty stupid fellas; the revelation that makes the joke work is that the second fella is far stupider (yet in an oddly logical way) than you ever dreamed. The twist casts their comical stupidity in a whole new light and forces you to re-evaluate what you've already assumed about the situation—but it is not a cheat. You haven't fallen off a cliff that you didn't know was there; rather, your eyes have been opened to the revelation that what you thought was solid ground is actually thin air.

A good joke, like a successful piece of longer humor or a good essay, finds its revelation within the material. That's the unity that makes it work, that leads the audience to laugh or cry.

Unity + revelation = humor that works

To see how unity and revelation help make a humor piece more than the sum of its parts (sound familiar?), let's look at a light, little back-of-the-book column I wrote for *Milwaukee Magazine*.

The focus of the piece was on how sports rivalries can cause disputes in even the happiest families; because our family had moved a lot, adopting new team loyalties with each new city, we'd had plenty of opportunities to spark fan friction with, in particular, my in-laws. On the surface, the point I pretended to be making was that all these family sports feuds were the fault of my in-laws, not us. The revelation running throughout, however, was that we were as much to blame for "The Rooting of All Evil" (as the story was titled) as anybody—perhaps more so. And the fact that, as we'd moved, we'd switched our own fan loyalties willy-nilly underscored the ultimate insignificance of this subject that we were nonetheless willing to split the family over. (I told you that conflict and contrast would come in handy in structuring such stories!)

I set up the situation and telegraphed my self-deprecating subtext right from the start:

> I was always taught that the two subjects one never brings up in polite conversation are politics and religion. Nobody warned me about sports.
>
> In fact, our family can agree to disagree even about politics and religion. For example, I'll cheerfully agree that my in-laws are political troglodytes who make Genghis Khan look like Alan Alda. No problems there, unless you count a few drumsticks hurled at each other across the Thanksgiving table. No, it's *sports* that has brought our otherwise-civilized clan almost to blows. Conflicting loyalties have set parent against child, brother against sister. Even our cat has been known to express contrary opinions.

The exaggeration and irony of my "cheerful" barb against my in-laws signals what's to come: While seemingly pointing a finger at my relatives' sports craziness, I will in reality be making fun of my own fanaticism (and, by extension, overzealous sports rivalries in general).

Two points are worth noting here that you'll find useful in constructing your own humorous articles. One is that, in general, in a humor piece the revelation builds throughout the article, rather than coming in a single punch line at the end, as in a joke. The revelation may be sharpest at the end, or you may reserve some final twist for the finish, but going for a single punch line in a supposedly humorous piece is asking a lot of the reader's patience. It's like telling a *very* long joke. (Conversely, as we will see in the next example, the revelation in an essay—where the reader is not expecting a punch line—can comfortably come singly and at the end.)

The second point you should remember is that the best target of a humorous article is yourself. While you may make fun of the foolish and the faddish, it will go down much better if you wear the foolishness and faddishness yourself, rather than taking shots at others. Study the work of humorist Dave Barry if you doubt this; the butt of Barry's humor, at least on the surface, is always Dave Barry.

In my sports-rivalry piece, for instance, I went on to explain why our family had so much trouble with this (our frequent moving) and doled out specific examples of sports-fueled family squabbles. Throughout, the chief culprit in fan excess always turned out to be me, despite my ironic take on the facts:

> . . . Somehow our battles over baseball—a more genteel, highbrow sport—remain on a higher plane, rarely stooping to shoving ballpark peanuts up each other's nostrils or pouring beer into in-laws' underwear. . . .
>
> . . . My sister-in-law, whose boyfriend went to Georgetown and somehow infected her with that allegiance, turned into the Hoya Fan from Hell when I worked at rival Pitt. . . . Please note that my wife and I are utterly blameless in all this unsportsmanlike conduct. Sewing a Pitt cheerleader outfit for our daughter and teaching her to spell out "H-O-Y-A-S S-T-I-N-K" doesn't count.

I described how even my daughter, born in Iowa as a Cubs fan, fell afoul of this mania when we moved to Pittsburgh and she refused to switch her loyalties as I had done:

Not that we pressured her, except for that little incident when we tried to throw out all her clothes that weren't Pirates black-and-gold. We handled this like mature adults, of course, calmly vowing to send our grade-school-age daughter out to spend the rest of the game in the stadium parking lot if she shouted "LET'S GO CUBS!" one more time. (She met a lot of interesting people out in the parking lot, by the way, and we're pretty sure that tattoo will fade before she gets to high school.)

By upping the irony as the piece went along—going from my in-laws to my even more blameless child—I built up to the closing ironic exaggeration. In the ending, I took all that had gone before and blew it up like a balloon until it popped and I'd punctured the silliness of getting so worked up over a game:

I can't explain why sports, of all things, so inflames people's passions. I guess I could engage in some windy dissertation on the sociocultural legacy of Roman gladiatorial contests, or sport as subliminated aggression. But I don't think that's it. No, I think it comes down to the basic laws of the universe—like gravity or how a slice of bread with peanut butter always lands sticky-side down.

That's right: The Brewers, Packers, Bucks, Panthers, Warriors and Badgers are simply *morally superior* to their foes. And I defy anyone to argue with me on that—at least until I start rooting for some other team.

That last qualification ("at least until I start rooting for some other team") was crucial to the puncturing. The ultra-exaggeration of "basic laws of the universe" and "moral superiority" took me right to the edge of the cliff; the final phrase pushed me off.

What gave those words their pushing power, their ability to reveal the total foolishness of all I'd been spouting, was how they sprang from what's gone before. Why is my family's sports rivalry problem so acute? Because we've moved and thus switched teams so often. Why is my claim that *my* teams are superior so ridiculous? Because the reader knows that my loyalties last only until the next moving van pulls up. It was unity that gave my little punch line its punch.

Using the richness of resonance

Another way of looking at the special unity that separates a good joke from a pointless non sequitur, or an effective essay from a meaningless ramble of words, is what I call *resonance*. In physics, resonance refers to the "reinforcement and prolongation of a sound by reflection or by vibration of other bodies." In humor or essay writing, what I mean by resonance is the reinforcement and enrichment of an idea or image by its reflection or echo later in the article. A really well-crafted article might have multiple ideas or images resonating throughout, like the verbal equivalent of ringing the changes on church bells.

In my little piece on sports fanaticism, for example, the ultimate puncturing of my "moral superiority" claims resonated with my fan fickleness, established in several places earlier in the article.

Often in humor pieces, in fact, something becomes funny by repetition. If you rolled out the whole joke the first time, the subsequent mention of a catchphrase or extension of the joke into a new realm echoes the original and generates far more humor than each iteration would by itself. (This is a common trick of situation comedies, too: If the family dog starts the sitcom humor by eating the Thanksgiving turkey, the later scene where the dog likewise eats the pumpkin pie intended for dessert becomes funnier by association.)

But resonance can be turned to more serious and subtle purposes, as well. In a well-structured essay the resonance created between two seemingly dissimilar ideas can lead to the revelation at the heart of the piece.

I tried to achieve something like this in another back-of-the-book article for *Milwaukee Magazine* in which I meditated on the slide of autumn into winter. Some people like spring the best of the seasons; I'm an autumn man myself, and as I thought about why I love this spectacular death of the year I made a link between the joys of fall and the pain of winter that follows it. Why do people in places like Milwaukee put up with winter, anyway?

Here's how I began the piece ("Falling Into Winter"), which ran in a January issue:

> I made some notes last fall, to help me remember how we got here from there. I wanted to record the long tumble from the first day of school, past Halloween, and into the leaden, leafless

days of November that lead inexorably—don't be fooled by the holiday tinsel—into brittle January. I figured that maybe it would make me feel better as I gloved the snow off my car (the scraper already broken) and crawled along a lakefront as gray as old silverware, only to head home again in Alaskan darkness. At least it would be cheaper than a week in Bermuda. . . .

From there I went through several examples of things I'd seen and enjoyed in autumn: the leaves along the riverbank, the last gasps of our garden, squirrels nibbling our Halloween pumpkins. In each case, the beauty of the season was tinged with signs of autumn's role in the ending of the year: "Leaves crimsoned overnight, as though they'd read that book on suicide, *Final Exit*, and decided to go out with a bang . . . ," our garden watermelons proved stillborn, the Halloween pumpkins perished. Each of these images was reinforced by resonance with the other, and with my opening on the "long tumble" into winter.

These smaller vignettes led up to a larger epiphany: a chance encounter, driving home from work one day, with "three deer, a mother and two fawns, crossing the road in a yellow-misted patch of light." I described the scene, ending with a phrase I hoped would resonate with my earlier notes of falling into darkness:

> I tapped the brakes to avoid spoiling this luminous moment by being rear-ended, then slowed to a stop. The deer, no more mindful of me in my red hunk of metal than of the dry leaves somersaulting across the grass, moseyed past my bumper and up onto a patch of green. As I crept forward, they bent to crop the grass a moment, then slid into the shadows.

Even though the deer, like the other glories of autumn I described, were bound to "slide into the shadows," I chose to focus on what Thoreau called "the tonic of wildness." Though the deer were pests to neighbors, I noted:

> . . . As a spectator, however, I can't help but be thankful for the deer and the small scene of grace they enacted at the end of my frantic day.

I used that sense of thankfulness, of autumn and such scenes as a gift, to launch my closing revelation (note the extra echo of the nibbling squirrels, by the way):

All of it made me think anew on what comes next—winter. It's not, as ministers hard up for a January sermon and refrigerator-door philosophers would have you believe, because of the expectation of spring. As a species, we're lousy at looking ahead; the squirrels gnawing our pumpkins have us clobbered in the foresight department. If we can see beyond next payday, we're latter-day Nostradamuses.

No, I think we put up with winter because autumn is such a gift. Guilt works on us far better than optimism: We enjoyed autumn and now we have to pay for it. Winter is the price for what Keats called the "season of mists and mellow fruitfulness."

And in the very end I called up one more note that I'd prepared for way back in my first paragraph, the notion of "cheaper than a week in Bermuda" (which, I hoped, would resonate with Milwaukeeans' renowned and self-proclaimed thriftiness). Here's how I wrapped it all up:

> Milwaukeeans—who cherish a good deal—are satisfied with this exchange. Keep giving us autumn and we'll bundle up when the bill comes due. Let them smirk down there in the seasonless Sun Belt. We know a bargain when we see one.

Unity made it all work, made the whole of my essay more than just a collection of autumn scenes. As each piece resonated with previous ideas and images, gaining depth and meaning in the echoes, the article built toward a revelation that turned the tables on the notion of darkness and decline. Of course we have to suffer winter after the gorgeous harvest of autumn! Nothing, not even autumn, comes without its price. But, oh, such a deal it is nonetheless.

Six tips for making it *look* easy

The tips you can draw from all this to better structure your humor and essays should be pretty obvious by now:

1. *Good structure is* more *important, not less, in such free-wheeling genres as humor and essay.* Plan your attack as though you were preparing for D-Day, even though the actual battle may more resemble Woodstock.

2. *Observe unity above all, making sure that everything you write*

contributes to the point you seek to make. Since you're making the rules here, there's no excuse for dragging in some surprise or gimmick out of left field.

3. *Decide what revelation you want to leave the reader with, and aim everything you write toward that end.* Think of your article as a joke: There'd better be a punch line, or watch out for the flying tomatoes from the audience.

4. *In a humor piece, don't save the whole revelation till the end (but do keep one last twist in your bag of carefully prepared-for tricks).* In an essay, where the reader's expectations are different, you can get away with saving the punch line for the very last.

5. *Plan for echoes.* Use resonance to bind your writing together and to make each element not only relate to others but gain weight from that relationship.

And let us not forget:

6. *It's not as easy as it looks!* But by paying careful attention to all that we've learned so far, you can craft humor and essays that make readers laugh, cry, and think differently about the world. Just remember that underlying the most seemingly artless and spontaneous writing is painstaking craft and relentless planning. The great ones make it *look* easy; that's what makes them great.

CHAPTER TWENTY-ONE

Longer Forms

Building a bigger bridge: From articles to books

Once you feel comfortable structuring and writing magazine articles, you may find yourself itching to tackle longer forms. You imagine your name running down the spine of a book. You envision going into a bookstore and finding your book on the shelves, shuffling it more to the front for better visibility if necessary (hey, don't laugh—I do it all the time!). You want to write the Great American Nonfiction Book.

Obviously, the regimen of focusing and organizing your writing that we've been exploring is even more crucial in an extended nonfiction project such as a book. You might be able to get away with knocking off a magazine article without a detailed plan (though obviously I don't recommend it!), but launching into a book without knowing exactly where you're headed and how you'll get there is like beginning a trip to the moon without a telescope or a star chart. A book is simply bigger than anyone can hold in his or her head, for one thing. For another, the peace of mind bought by planning ahead lets you tackle such a big project in manageable chunks; trying to grapple with a whole book all at once is paralyzing.

In making the leap from articles to books, the question is not whether to focus and outline but *how*: How do you extend the strategies of organizing, say, 3,000 words into a way of mapping out 70,000 words?

Remember how we likened the writing process to building a bridge? Your task as a nonfiction writer is to take readers from here to there and to keep them interested along the way so they don't jump off. A book represents a much longer bridge than a magazine article. At first, it might seem that you can build a book simply by taking what you'd put in a magazine article and stretching it over a longer span, but if you know much about bridges or books, you'll quickly see that such a scheme is bound to collapse.

The reason such an approach seems plausible is that the writing of every good magazine article inevitably leaves much of the writer's notebook unused. In plucking out only what fits your focus—and, to be practical, your assigned length—you may use just 20 percent of what you've written down. And what's in your notebook itself represents a careful culling of the total information you've run across in the course of your research. If you'd transcribed everything your sources said, copied every fact from your secondary sources . . . why, you'd have enough to fill a book!

So why not just write a book by taking everything you *could* have put into a magazine article and, well, putting it in? No one would want to read such a book, for one thing, and the truth is no one would really want to write it. A successful nonfiction book must be more than just a puffed-up magazine article; you left out all that stuff in writing the article for a reason, after all, not just because you didn't have enough pages.

While a book does allow you to explore a subject in far greater depth than a magazine article, the depth of your raw material must expand accordingly. To return to our bridge-building analogy, the book writer's task is not simply to stretch the same amount of steel and girders and cables over a greater space, ever thinner like a rubber band or a distended wad of chewing gum. No, the book writer must structure every part of the way with the same care and attention to detail that the magazine writer spends on a 2,000- or 3,000-word span.

Focusing wider, deeper

For the writer familiar with the principles of structure and flow, then, the challenge of a book-length project becomes first a question of focus. If part of the problem of planning an article is biting off no more than you can chew—focusing, in other words—the book writer must decide how to expand that focus into a feast.

Part of expanding your focus from an article into a book is widening it—but only part, and not necessarily the main part. A few chapters back, for instance, we imagined writing about wineries in and around Seattle. That's a good subject for a magazine article, but for a book-length project you might want to widen to encompass wineries of the entire Pacific Northwest. A story on "The Ten Best Educational Software Programs for Your Kids" might make a fine article for a family or a computer magazine. But that focus would be too narrow for a book, where you might choose to cover kids' software of all kinds (educational and purely entertainment, as well as the "edutainment" programs in-between) and where you might want to categorize your recommendations by particular age ranges. Similarly, a magazine profile touches on a far narrower slice of your subject's life than would a book-length biography.

But even these hypothetical examples suggest that changing your focus for a book-length project requires more than merely broadening your scope. You must also deepen and enrich it—using more steel, to return to our bridge-building metaphor.

If you took your outline for an article on Seattle wineries, say, and just tacked on a bunch more wineries, you'd have a long article—but well shy of a book. Your quick take on ten kids' computer programs, which seems so lively and breezy in a magazine form, would seem choppy and ultimately tedious if simply extended to one hundred programs.

To build a book on wineries of the Pacific Northwest, to continue that example, you'd need to go beyond adding more wineries, each written in the same way you'd round them up in a magazine article. You'd want to have a chapter setting the area's wine industry into context, perhaps, and maybe another chapter exploring the climate and geography (how, for example, the area resembles the wine-growing region of France). These are topics that you'd probably touch on in a magazine article—but in a paragraph or two each. A book allows you to take the same breadth of focus and delve much deeper. (Again, however, this is not just a matter of using a greater percentage of your notes. If you took thirty pages of notes for a magazine article and used the equivalent of six pages' worth, you might need to take thirty pages of notes for just one chapter on the same general topic—and you'd still use only a half-dozen pages or so.)

In addition to these overview, scene-setting chapters, your wineries book might have at its core a series of chapters that cover each part of the region, one by one, much as your original article explored the Seattle area. Each chapter would need at least as much depth and detail as your original article did. It's likely, in fact, that each chapter would be somewhat longer, richer and more in-depth than a magazine article. If your Seattle article found its way into the book, you'd probably find yourself adding to it, doing additional research and covering ground you missed the first time around.

Finding your focus

Wouldn't it be easier, you may be wondering by this point, just to widen your focus until it's big enough to fill a book? If the Pacific Northwest doesn't have enough wineries, why not throw in California too? If one hundred kids' computer programs don't make a book, cover one hundred great adult programs as well. Heck, that's about one per page, and you wouldn't have to do much more research than reading a bunch of computer catalogs!

The danger of such an approach is that eventually your book winds up with no focus at all. And focus isn't just a handy tool for structuring your story, remember; it's essential for reader interest. The more your book seems to be about everything, the more (from the book-buyer's standpoint) it's about nothing. As writer Katherine Krull has observed (quoted in *Good Advice on Writing*, by William Safire and Leonard Safir), "More often, narrowing the focus of your book may paradoxically increase the number of people who will actually buy it. Narrowing your focus can improve your writing as well, and make your book better overall."

A book needs a focus as much or more than a magazine article does, and the more sharply you define that focus the easier it will be to research and write. The shape of your book must grow out of that focus, rather than pulling an unfocused glob of material together and calling it a book.

Although a book on wineries of a particular region might seem to be little more than a series of magazine articles cobbled together as chapters, a book that actually grows that way won't be much of a book. It might be a very good compilation, but it will never be more than a compilation. Such a book is unlikely to achieve that goal we keep setting: to be more than the sum of its parts.

Rather, a book must spin out from its essential focus, its structure growing ever more intricate and detailed like the spinning of a spider's web. A spider doesn't make a web by pasting together chunks of smaller webs. And the focus of the spider's web, no matter how lovely and large it becomes, always remains singular: to catch a fly.

Growing a book outline

Let's see how our make-believe book on wineries might be spun out of this focus: the Pacific Northwest as America's answer to Bordeaux. That notion immediately leads to two corollary ideas: 1. The similarities, in terms of what matters to wine growing, between the Pacific Northwest and the wine-growing heart of France; and 2. The comparison and contrast to what most readers already think of as America's chief claim to wine fame, the Napa and Sonoma valleys of California.

As we begin to outline the book, we might start with these ideas and break them out into some possible chapters or subchapters:

Pacific Northwest overview

Elements for successful wine-growing

Pacific Northwest wine-growing climate, similarities to France

Pacific Northwest wine-growing soil and other factors, similarities to France

History of Pacific Northwest wine, how it started much later than California

Recent boom in Pacific Northwest wine, gaining on California

From there, we'd probably want to launch into a series of chapters organized by geography. After all, we've already established geography as a key part of the book's focus, so a region-by-region tour of wineries makes sense. We could logically order the geographic sections by the map (north to south, west to east . . .), or, since we've introduced history and the growth of the region's wine industry as an element, we could go from the areas where the wine business began to the newer frontiers of Pacific Northwest viticulture. Taking the former approach, our rough outline might continue:

Oregon's Umpqua Valley
Oregon's Willamette Valley
Washington's Columbia Valley
Washington's Yakima Valley

And so on, leading readers from the part of Oregon closest to California (significant in our focus), north through Washington and then east to cover Idaho.

By the time we covered all the wine-growing sections within our focus, and then perhaps added a final chapter on the future of Pacific Northwest wine, we'd have the rough plan of a book. From our one focus came three sub-focuses, not necessarily equal in importance but all necessary to do the job at hand: climate and geography compared to France, history and industry compared to California, plus the large chunk on the actual wineries, organized by geography. These three main parts of the book then became a dozen or more chapters.

Next you would structure each chapter much the way you would a magazine article. The exact length and number of chapters pretty much boils down to math: If your book is 75,000 words, you'll need thirty chapters the length of a short magazine article (2,500 words), or sixteen chapters the length of a longish article (4,500 words). Or some combination in-between. Once you have a feel for how many chapters your book breaks into, and the relative length required for each, you can roughly apportion the words to reach your intended total.

Your book's outline thus grows from one focus to a handful of elements to a list of chapters to a detailed fleshing out of every chapter. And suddenly you have a whole book mapped out.

It's not essential, however, to have every chapter completely outlined before you begin writing chapter one. You should also expect to change and refine your structure in progress—even dropping or adding whole chapters—more than you might with a simpler, short-term project such as a magazine article. The important thing is to have a clear focus and a sense of what you will cover in each chapter (as well as, equally important, what you expect *not* to cover). You need to know where your book is going and enough of how you'll get there to set off with complete confidence in your ability to complete the journey.

Trust me, you can do it. Look at me—I'm just one chapter away from completing this book!

CHAPTER TWENTY-TWO

Revising

Structure vs. polish

I've put off this chapter till last not just because last is where it logically fits—revising, after all, is the writer's final task before popping a manuscript in the mail—but also because, unlike almost everything that's come before, revising is not a topic near and dear to my heart. If a big fat contract landed in my mailbox with the chance to earn millions writing a whole book on revising (a sure bestseller, say, "Sex and the Second Draft" or "Valley of the Rewrites"), I'd have to pass.

It's not that I don't believe in polishing your writing, or think it's unimportant. I just don't find the need to spend much time or creative energy on revising—because, frankly, my first drafts come out darn near ready for the typesetter.

That's not bragging: My first drafts are better than many writers' third drafts because, as we've seen all through this book, I prefer to invest my time and creativity up front rather than after one whole set of words has been committed to paper. You can make the same boast if you do your homework on structure and flow before you start writing and then pay attention to your outline when you're at the keyboard. If you find yourself tearing up your work and reassembling it after it's written, you don't need a chapter on revising—you need to go back to the start of this book.

Moreover, in the grand scheme of things, getting your structure right is simply more important than polishing each sentence six times. It's like the difference between building a house from a good blueprint and making sure that the paint in your living room precisely matches the roses in your bathroom wallpaper; both are desirable, but if the roof falls down the wallpaper hue won't much matter.

As Jon Franklin puts it in *Writing for Story*, "The brutal fact is that structure is far more fundamental to storytelling than polish. . . . Readers will buy story without polish, but I defy you to find a best-seller that has polish without story."

And even when revising, the most important work comes down to questions of form and organization. Your first job in taking a hard look at your first draft has to be making sure the roof won't fall down on the reader's head. As William Zinsser says of his own work in *On Writing Well*, "My revisions aren't the best ones that could be made, or the only ones. They're mainly matters of carpentry: fixing the structure and the flow. . . . Most rewriting is a matter of juggling elements that already exist. And I'm not just talking about individual sentences. The total construction is equally important."

So what *does* the well-structured writer need to look for in revising? Let's put those wallpaper samples aside for a moment and take one last look at the nuts and bolts. . . .

Your revision checklist

As you read through your own work, it helps to have a sort of check-list—whether written or just in your head—to make sure that you've built something that will hold up to somebody else's reading. Here are some key questions to ask as you revise:

1. *Does the lead grab the reader? Does the lead flow smoothly into the rest of the story?* Remember that by now you know far more about your topic than the reader. Try to read your opening paragraphs with fresh eyes: Are they crafted to intrigue someone coming to this subject without your passion and acquired expertise? Then make certain that the attractive road you've started the reader down doesn't lead off a cliff—your lead has to lead somewhere, seamlessly flowing into the body of the story. If there's a dropoff where the lead ends and the "real" article begins, you need to do some repairs. (It's even possible

that your lead doesn't spring naturally from the focus of your story, that it's one of those tacked-on come-ons we warned against back in chapter ten. If so, go back to the heart of your story and look again for your real lead: It may be buried in the body of your article and need only promoting to the start of your story.)

2. *Can you summarize your focus and angle in a headline and subhead?* It's easy to lose track of your main idea as you spin out a story; on rereading, make certain that your focus remains as sharp and clear as when you started. If you came up with a mock headline and subhead as part of structuring the story, check them against the actual first draft: Do they still fit? Or did you let the story wander from its *raison d'etre*?

3. *Are your focus and angle clearly encapsulated in your hook? Is your hook high enough?* The reason for double-checking your focus right after the lead, after all, is that your hook had better reflect that focus—and soon. As you examine the clarity of your hook, check too to make sure it comes early enough in the article. Buried hooks are the bane of editors and readers; on the other hand, it's almost impossible to plant your hook *too* high in the story. Don't forget that your patience for reaching the "who cares?" element of your own article will far exceed the reader's.

4. *Does each paragraph or section flow easily into the next?* Here's the time to test all your transitions. Seek out and destroy any interruption in the flow of your story. Rough transitions may be simply a sign of poor linking between paragraphs—fixable by tweaking a few words or switching a phrase—or they may be a red flag signaling something's out of place. If you can't make a chunk of information fit smoothly into your flow at a given point, maybe it doesn't belong there. See if the sore-thumb section fits more naturally and logically elsewhere in your article. And check it against your focus: Maybe the right cure is surgery—just cut it out.

5. *Does your logic hold together?* Your article doesn't have to pass a logician's inspection, but now is the time to make sure your arguments hold water and your assertions are properly supported. Examine each point you make with these questions in mind: Does what comes next logically follow (the dreaded non sequitur)? Does the evidence you present actually support your point? Look for logical leaps and factual holes, for what lawyers call "assuming facts not in evidence."

Have you left out something that "everybody knows" when "everybody" really doesn't? Do you introduce new terms and ideas at the proper points, or must the reader read backward to understand what you're saying?

6. *Does everything read as if it belongs to the same article?* In short, do a unity check. This means being alert to nuances of tone and style as well as spotting content that simply doesn't belong. In a piece that you hope the reader will want to read at one sitting, make sure that it reads as though it was *written* at one sitting—even if you painstakingly crafted the article in bits and pieces over days or weeks. More glaringly, look for paragraphs or whole section detours that seem, on rereading, simply "dropped from space," as a friend of mine likes to put it. If you find yourself wondering, "Where the heck did this come from?" or "Why is this in here?" hit the "delete" key, hard.

7. *Within the article, is everything that belongs together placed together?* If you're covering points A, B, C and D, do you say everything you need to say about C in one spot, or are little bits of C scattered throughout the article? Would your organization hold up under the close scrutiny of a fifth-grade teacher bent on impressing students with the holy obligations of outlining? Putting all the stuff that belongs together under the same organizational umbrella is one of an editor's most common and most burdensome tasks. Your outline, if you built it right and stuck to it, should have eliminated most of these editing sore spots; now's the time to make sure.

Some bits of your main points will wind up elsewhere in your article, of course, to do the work of your lead, hook and even ending. You might need to use an example from C in your lead and another in your hook. But everything else about C belongs in your C section—not scattered here and there in the A, B and D portions. (Here's where rocky transitions may warn you that something is out of place.)

8. *Does the rhythm move the reader along?* Look at both your overall, larger rhythms and the individual rhythms of sentences and paragraphs. Watch out for a pace that's too breathless, or too languid. You'll need built-in resting places for the reader—but not too many, or too long. You'll want to build to a climax or sense of reader satisfaction, but don't take too long in getting there or get there too early (with too long an aftermath before your ending).

Within the larger rhythms of your writing, check for sentences that run on too long or sentences that seem too staccato. The same goes for paragraphs: After a series of long paragraphs, give the reader a break; too many short paragraphs placed one after another, on the other hand, can be just as wearying. Variety is the key to making your rhythm work.

Check particularly the rhythm of your quotes. Have you strung one quote after another, subjecting readers to more of a monologue than an article? Remember that your job as a nonfiction writer is to select and filter the raw stuff of an interview, placing quotes in context and making them part of a larger whole. Don't shirk your duty and just let your subjects ramble on in print! At the other extreme, be on the lookout for chopped-up quotes and partial quotations. Too many tiny chunks of words between quotation marks means you should either let the poor guy talk or go ahead and paraphrase all the way.

Rhythm is one of the hardest things to get right in your first draft, because it so depends on a final effect that can only be gauged as a whole. But breaking up or combining sentences and paragraphs, quotes and paraphrases can be both the easiest and the most effective revising you do.

9. *Does your chronology track?* Test your first draft to see how many twists and turns in the sequence of events you force the reader to follow. If you have more than one flashback, more than a single loop in time, you're probably asking for trouble—and confusion. Review the tenses you employ in each stage of the story, looking for elements out of sequence. Be ruthless with unnecessary backtracking. Try charting your chronology as it happened in time, then comparing this list to the order of events in your story: An article that begins *in medias res* and then catches up to itself (E-F-G-A-B-C-D-H . . .) is OK—just don't risk a second loop in time. But seemingly random insertions of elements out of chronological order (A-B-C-H-D-E-Q-F . . .) are pure poison to reader flow.

10. *Is your order consistent?* This is a small point, but it can drive the reader crazy. For example, if your hook promises that you will explore three important new developments in computer graphics—A, B and C, listed in that order—your story should not then proceed C-B-A. If your lead entices readers with tidbits about four Caribbean islands—Barbados, Antigua, Jamaica and St. Thomas, in that order—you should deliver the goods in the body of your article in that same

sequence, unless there's a mighty good reason for doing otherwise.

11. *Does your ending tie it all together?* Some stories can just stop, but only when all that's come before leads to a conclusion that's not only natural and logical but that supports the story's focus. Other articles demand a more overt ending strategy that hammers home your main thesis. And some can even have surprise endings—but the surprise should never be truly out of the blue. Rather it should be a revelation that makes all the previous material more meaningful and whole.

Check your ending against your hook: Have you delivered what you promised high up in the story? Test the ending, too, against your lead: Have you brought the reader to a destination that fits with the start of your journey together?

12. *Have you written to the right length?* In the world of nonfiction publishing, pages equal dollars. Editors frown on writers who regularly turn in copy that's the wrong length (usually too long, seldom too short), and keep coming back to those who consistently deliver the goods as ordered. Rigorous pruning of extraneous material at every step of the writing process, plus regular counting of words-so-far as you write the first draft, will help you finish your first draft within striking distance of your desired length. But often you'll wind up a little long. Surgical removal of extra adjectives and adverbs and general tightening of your prose can usually solve the problem, but sometimes you need to tinker with your structure to reach the right length.

If you've followed your outline, it should be easier to identify which chunks can be removed or radically condensed without damage to the whole. You may even need to reshuffle a few pieces to make sure they fit your altered organizational scheme. That's OK—your outline is a map, not a straitjacket.

Remember my "virtual travel" story from back in chapter nineteen? In my original outline, I had a small chunk about a *Star Trek* attraction opening at a Las Vegas hotel; I'd placed this at the end, to play off the *Star Trek* image in my lead. Once the actual article was almost done, however, I realized that it was running over its (pretty puny) word allotment. Studying my outline, I was able to identify an earlier, just as suitable spot for the story to end: with a look to the future of "virtual travel." So I lopped off the *Star Trek* ending and settled on the conclusion that you saw in chapter nineteen.

Sometimes you will need to do this kind of structural surgery. Even though I hate to revise, I occasionally wind up scribbling anew on my already-scribbly outline, drawing arrows and crossing out earlier notations. But if you have an outline—if the overall structure of your "house" is sound—you'll know exactly which parts are "bearing walls" and which can stand remodeling. A sense of structure and flow can go a long way toward limiting the amont of revising you need to do in the first place—and it can give you a blueprint for the revisions that you need to make even so.

The art of nonfiction

When you finish revising with an eye to structure and flow, the raw material that you began with, way back at the first focusing of your idea into an article, will have a new shape. You will have taken a chunk of the unstructured stuff of the world and formed it into something with meaning and purpose—made a diamond out of coal, to return to our very first image of what this process is all about. The raw material is out there for anyone to see, but the structure you create and the meaning with which you infuse it are uniquely yours.

That's a pretty good summary of the whole human adventure: making meaning out of chaos. The nonfiction writer's challenge—and the nonfiction writer's joy—lies in doing something that is so fundamental to the human spirit and in doing it in a way no one else can. When you can see that the difference between coal and diamonds is structure, not substance, you understand that the art lies not in the raw material but within the artist—you.

INDEX